Prayer Partners
with Jesus

Brian Simmons

insight *i* publishing group

Tulsa, Oklahoma

PRAYER PARTNERS WITH JESUS

Prayer Partners with Jesus by Brian Simmons
Published by Insight Publishing Group
8801 S. Yale, Suite 410
Tulsa, OK 74137
918-493-1718

Unless otherwise noted all scripture quotations are taken from the New International Version of the Bible. Copyright © 1973, 1978, 1984 by International Bible Society. Used by permission of Zondervan Publishing House. Scripture quotations marked NAS are taken from the New American Standard Bible. Copyright © 1960, 1962, 1963, 1968, 1971, 1972, 1973, 1975, 1977, 1995 by the Lockman Foundation. Used by permission.

ISBN 1-930027-85-0

Library of Congress catalog card number: 2002115913

Printed in the United States of America

Dedication

To Every Praying Believer
Who Longs to Become
A Prayer Partner with the Son of God

And

To the One Person Who
Has Taught Me More About
Prayer Than Any One on Earth…
My Beloved Wife—Candy

"Finally brothers, pray for us that the message of the Lord may spread rapidly and be honored, just as it was with you" (II Thessalonians 3:1)

Contents

Preface

Like most Christians, I have struggled through a prayer journey with typical highs and lows. There have been days recently that I really thought I could pray without stopping—it is becoming sheer joy to be with HIM, pouring out my heart. In my journey with Jesus, I am learning to lean on my Beloved and become a prayer partner with Jesus, my Friend. _He_ has become "my prayer life." These notes reflect this process. . . .

Many have made rich deposits in my life, teaching me about prayer. A dear brother was led by God in the first months of my walk with Jesus to be a prayer partner with me. Bob Bence, from Augusta, Kansas, will always be a praying friend to me. Many testify of the presence of the Lord released when Bob enters the room. He taught me I could pray at anytime with bold faith and with tears! Duane Stous, Jim Ostewig, Robert Kaminsky, Clarence Preedy—Bible school professors with New Tribes Mission who lived what they taught me about prayer. My dear Kuna friends in the church of Pucuro, Panama. I will never forget your prayers that brought healing to me as I lay dying of amoebic dysentery in the jungle! Many friends in many places with many differing styles of prayer, yet they all impacted me deeply.

Three men stand out to me as powerful examples of praying men: Mike Bickle, a busy servant of God, who has made prayer and fasting a lifestyle; James Goll, who has taken a leap into the deep waters of intercession and the secrets of prayer power; and Lou Engle, a friend who has released more through his prayers than any man I know. I am so thankful that Mike, James, and Lou "come up for air" long enough to tell the rest of us what they are learning!

But beyond these three, there is another who has helped me in this prayer journey . . . my treasure and friend, <u>Candy</u>. I have seen in her, a ceaseless spirit of prayer that both convicts me and soothes my soul at the same time. She has followed me to the ends of the earth as a covenant partner in ministry. How could I even speak of my love for her? Candy has shown me that Jesus loves to hear us pray! What a prayer partner she is to me!

In this study you will be taught about the basics of prayer, warfare, and intercession. Apply your heart to all that you read. Look up all the verses we cover. Take notes and go deep. The more you give to this study, the more you will receive. Start by praying this prayer with me:

> ***Dear Lord Jesus,*** *You know I love You. You know I want to become a person of prayer. Teach me to pray. Help me when I don't feel like praying to remember how You prayed in the garden of Gethsemane. I give myself to You to be taught to pray. Change my life as I learn to make prayer my joy. Give me the prayer assignments you want me to have. I give myself to You. I call You my Friend and Lover of My Soul. Impart Your grace to my life as You make me Your prayer partner. In Jesus' name—Amen.*

Now let's go for it! Expect incredible things to happen to <u>you</u>, as you become a ***Prayer Partner with the Son of God!*** What you are about to read is the expression of my heart. Words that I trust will benefit new believers in giving them a "fast-start" in their prayer journey. For the experienced, you will want to spend more time on the later chapters. Wherever you are in YOUR JOURNEY— our prayer is that you will find a <u>booster-rocket</u> in these pages that will shoot you right into the glory clouds of prayer. May you have a good ride! Enjoy the view. Hope you don't mind high places!

Brian Simmons

Thirsting for God

❖ ❖ ❖ ❖ ❖

As the deer pants for streams of water,
So my soul pants for you O God.
Psalm 42:1

I'm on a quest to discover how to teach people on prayer without leaving them defeated and feeling ashamed. There are none of us who really prays enough, yet I don't see Jesus in the Bible going around making everybody feel lousy and condemned about *not* praying. He just told His disciples, *"When you pray"*—not, "Why don't you pray more, you clod!" Somehow I sense our Lord Jesus understands the battle we go through in developing a life of prayer.

"Your voice is sweet."—*Song of Songs 2:14*

Where is there condemnation in that?

No one is good enough to pray. But the God revealed by Jesus listens to you. I am convinced that guilt is the greatest hindrance to prayer. Guilt is a poor motivator in the Christian life. Guilt *will* produce results—for a while—that is, until we realize that guilt leaves an aftertaste in our soul. You probably will never pray enough; you will probably never pray perfectly with the right passion and the right words, etc. But still there is sweetness to our voice in the ears of Jesus Christ. "Come and pray to me," He says, "Let me hear your voice in prayer!"

It's time to invade the privacy of God and rush into His presence like a child and love on Him. So, here's my teaching on prayer. I hope its fat (guilt) free.

Everything about you was made for God.

You were created to need His presence. The true longing of your heart is to know Him, for you were formed in His image. Prayer is expressing this soul-thirst for God. We come alive when we come before our True Source. The human spirit is empowered by prayer. Absolutely nothing else compares to being with Him!

The purpose of living is to be God's vessel, filled with His life. He becomes our content—our substance—and we become His container. Without man God has nowhere to put Himself, nowhere to pour out His very life. He can fill the universe with His wisdom and order, but He longs for a home, a place to pour out His life. In a very real way, God needs you. You become His completion, His fullness on the earth. See Ephesians 1:17-23.

Thirsting for God is the soul's desire to connect with the eternal. Like a hunted deer panting for refreshment, we thirst for the living God. This thirst can sometimes be overwhelming. We just can't go on without a fresh infilling from the Fountain of Life. Prayer gives us that infilling.

Prayer is God's gift to us.

It is His way of drawing us into His heart. He knows that life-changing power is released when we spend time with Jesus in prayer. Adoration turns into transformation if we will be patient. To love Him is our supreme occupation. The more we love Him; the more we spend time with Him, and the more we spend time with Him, the more our soul is transformed into His image (II Cor. 3:18, John 14:21). As we give Him our heart in prayer, He gives us His heart in exchange, transforming us deep within.

It is true that God will change you through prayer. We breathe together, God and man. His life changes us forever. The more you pray, the more you are filled with God.

As you offer your heart to Him, the Holy Spirit takes the Word of God and renews your mind. As you pray, have the Bible open. Read, and then pray. Pray, and then read. You will be surprised at how rich the Word will become as Jesus opens the eyes of your understanding (Luke 24: 45).

Think of the Holy of Holies
As the heart of the Father.

Now, think of the veil separating you from the Holy of Holies as being torn open by the Father's hand. Think of God's heart being torn open for you to peek into, and see that He really is kind and merciful and forgiving after all—not for the few, but for YOU! Prayer is the exquisite privilege of looking at God. He is not a marble figure like a statue staring at you, wondering why it took you so long; He is a Father with a heart torn open ready to receive you and hear your voice cry out to Him. He loves it!

Why do we pray?

Have you ever considered the mystery of prayer? We tell God what He tells us to tell Him, and ask Him for what He already knows we have need of. Yet this is the way God draws us into partnership with Him in fulfilling

His purposes on the earth. It is both simple and profound. Prayer has affected human history more than can be calculated. Prayer is a divine, sacred, glorious mystery that will draw us into His heart. Prayer is a privilege—the opportunity to lock arms with God as we labor together.

Prayer is life taken to its *highest degree.* Prayer takes us into the timelessness of His presence to speak with God and hear His heart. Did you know there are over 600 prayers in the Bible? And that does not count the 150 Psalms, which are prayers that are sung. Here are some reasons why you must become a Prayer Partner with Jesus:

1. *Prayer Is the Love-Link Between Friends.*

Only a Lover-Friend will always be there to hear our cry. It is true: Jesus will never leave you; He will never fail you. We cry out to Him because our heart is lovesick for the Son of God! Until we see Him face to face, we learn of His kindness through prayer. He loves to hear our cry, and we love to spend time with Him.

We must be those who seek His presence, not just His presents. The Lord's Prayer begins with "Our Father," not "Our needs." Worship, not whining, is the highest form of prayer. As we pray, our friendship with the **Beloved One** deepens and sweetens as the true needs of our heart are answered by loving Him. Read Song of Songs 2:14.

2. *Prayer Was the Priority of Jesus.*

Many mornings, Jesus began with prayer in solitude. Jesus was in prayer when the Holy Spirit came upon Him at His baptism. Jesus received power, wisdom, and strategy by His intimate prayer life with the Father.

Over twenty-five times in the gospels we see Jesus in prayer. Even during the last hours of His life He prayed. Everything about the ministry of our Lord Jesus was rooted in prayer. May we have the same longing for time alone with the Father as Jesus did.

If it was a priority to the Holy Son of God to live continually in the presence of His Father, so must we (fallen ones) seek Him continually. The very prayer habits of our Lord Jesus will be repeated on earth by a new breed of praying pioneers who seek Him above everything else. Jesus is the perfect prayer partner for you. Read Matthew 14:23, Mark 1:35, Luke 6:12.

3. *Prayer Is our Ministry unto the Lord.*

We pray not only to receive what we need, but to KNOW HIM. All prayer is a union with God. We join our heart, our spirit, and our longings with God's—touching the eternal together. Our hearts are drawn out toward heaven when we open our lips and call upon His Name. Any need we have must be secondary to satisfying His Father-heart in prayer.

You are a priest coming to God with words, a priest with a ministry before the throne. Prayer is the greatest and noblest human action possible. Our true ministry is not what we do before others, but who we are before the Lord (I Peter 2:5-9).

4. *Prayer Opens our Spiritual Eyes.*

God's Spirit can open blind eyes. We are all born blind because of sin. Only the Holy Spirit can cause us to see as we pray. True spiritual insight comes with a humble desire to know Jesus. Many things will be shown to you as you pray. Expect your eyes to be opened to see into the spiritual realm all around you.

The kingdom of heaven is at hand, close enough to reach. Sacred secrets will be shared with you as you make Jesus your lifetime prayer partner. Pray that God will open your eyes to see the glory of Christ! (II Kings 6:16-17, Eph. 1:17-18, and I Cor. 2:9-10.)

5. *Prayer Is a Love Response to Others.*

Every true prayer partner with Jesus will learn to carry the concerns of others. When we understand how powerful prayer is, we will pray forcefully for God's best to come to others. Prayer can lift their burdens, just as it lifts yours.

To pray for another is one of the most loving things you can do. As you grow in love, you will grow in your prayer response to the burdens of your friends. Ask the Lord today to show you how to pray for others and watch miracles come to them! (Phil. 1:7).

6. Prayer Escorts God's Will to the Earth.

The ministry of prayer is to bring the will of heaven to earth. We stand on God's side wanting what God wants. Our prayers paint a "bulls-eye" for the next place where God's power will fall. True prayer is discovering God's heart as we draw near to Him and then joining Him in intercession until His will is done on earth as it is in heaven. When you know what is happening in heaven, you can pray it done on earth (Amos 3:7).

True prayer is Christ in you praying through you to accomplish the Father's desires for the earth. It is true: Jesus Christ is your prayer partner, and He will pray through you as you pray through Him! It is by your prayers that God takes charge of things on earth.

The highest privilege of the Church is to be the outlet of God's will. Our praying gives us the holy privilege of escorting God's purposes to the earth. Pull down the future into the present with your prayer of faith. Try it! Read Matthew 6:10, and Psalm 119:126.

7. Prayer Releases Miracle Power.

Wherever you see miracles, you will find prayer. God releases miracles in answer to the prayers of His people. YOU are one who can pray down the miracle power of heaven. We do not "hype" it up; we pray it down! More prayer—more power. Without prayer, we cannot do the works of Jesus, let alone the "greater" things He claimed we would do. Miracles are waiting for your prayers.

Bold prayer brings big miracles. It is time for you to pray! Don't let everybody else see the miracles without YOU being included! Read Luke 5:15-16, and John 14:12-14.

8. Prayer Is a Weapon of Spiritual Warfare.

There is nothing more powerful in your arsenal than "believing prayer." It will push back the enemies of righteousness like nothing else. We have a potent, dynamic weapon in our mouths—the prayer of faith! If you truly wish to see victory in your life over the things that disturb the Holy Spirit, you must take up the weapons of prayer.

Divine weapons will never fail you. The devil is continually plotting your fall. Only the weapon of persistent and overcoming prayer will deliver you. The devil runs when you pray. Prayer enables the weakest believer to break through into victory and deliverance. Never underestimate the potency of your prayers! Read Ephesians 6:10-18.

9. *Prayer Brings Peace, Comfort, and Joy.*

Most of us carry burdens that must be given up and laid aside (Phil. 4:6-7). Prayer from the heart is like dialing 911. It is God's system for emergency response. Yes, He knows what you need before you ask, but by asking, our hearts turn to our true source of life, comfort, and peace. Nothing soothes the heart like prayer (James 5:13).

Just as parents are stirred by the cry of their children, so Abba (Father God) is moved by your sigh. He is touched by the feeling of your weakness and understands you more than you realize (Heb. 4:15-16). As we pour out our hearts before Him, we touch the flow of compassion in Father's heart (Isa. 30:19). Read Psalms 61-63 and underline the references to prayer and the results of prayer!

10. *Prayer Is How We Receive What We Need.*

Simply stated, we do not have what we need because we do not ask for it (James 4:2). Asking and receiving is the dynamic of prayer that relieves the pain of life and releases the substance of heaven. Whatever we need, whenever we need it, we simply ask the Father to give it. This cultivates our relationship as children of God. Just as earthly fathers delight in caring for and providing for their children—so our heavenly Father knows what we have need of and will give it when we ask.

Jesus once said to blind Bartimaeus, "What do you want me to do for you?" Jesus is still saying this to every blind beggar who comes to Him. Do you have a need? Is there a burden on your heart? Is there something you want that only God can give you? Ask and He will answer!

Types of Prayer

The Lord loves diversity. That is why He made us all different with different ways of viewing life. God has the wonderful ability to understand all of us when we pray with different needs. There are many types of prayer in the Bible. You can come to God in a hundred different ways and still not exhaust them all. We have listed five major categories of prayer:

1. Praise, Adoration, and Thanksgiving

Praise is God's address. If you cannot find God, praise Him and He will show up! Begin your encounter with God in prayer with extended seasons of praise. It is OK to be loud and rowdy, and it is fine if you simply want to be quiet and reflective. Nevertheless, praise the Lord, all you servants of His!

Adoration is a form of intimate worship. Tell the Lord you adore Him. Look long at His beauty. Close your eyes and speak it out, "Jesus, I adore YOU." Then, you can **thank Him** all day long for what He means to you. Isn't that simple? This is the kind of praying that will free your heart from anxiety and care. As we become "thankful praisers," peace enters our heart (Phil. 4:6-7).

2. Confession

We all fail to live perfectly before God. We must have a fresh start, a chance to begin afresh—a "do-over," a rebound. When you confess your sins honestly before a loving, caring Father, He forgives and lets you start over with a spiritual rebound.

Think about it. How can He be holy and put up with sinful people like us? Because Jesus took away all our sins. Confession forces us into the place of honesty where mercy pierces us again. Be quick to confess, and He will be quick to forgive you! (I John 1:9, Mic. 7:19).

3. Asking

The simplest prayer of all is "Please God, do this for me." Our God is a prayer-answering God. He will not hesitate to answer the cry of those who love Him and ask in faith. Keep God busy answering your prayers—He won't mind. Let Him know what you need. Be a holy reminder to the Lord. The more you ask, the more you will receive. Prayer is God's way of receiving what we need.

Keep on *asking*, keep on *seeking*, keep on *knocking*, and the door of answered prayer will be opened for you (Matt. 7:7-11). Go ahead, run into God's presence and invade the privacy of God! See yourself as a five-year-old who rushes into the Father's presence, oblivious of manners. Your Father can handle it. He is Abba!

4. Intercession

This is asking God to intervene as we plead before God on behalf of others. Sometimes it involves groups of people praying together (corporate prayer). Intercession is the ministry of every believer. When we come to the Lord on behalf of someone else, we are interceding for them. You have the priestly ministry of begging God to touch others (I Tim. 2:1-3). This stretches your heart in love. We will share about his latter in the book.

5. Warfare

Warfare prayer is taking hold of an intruder and binding him tight so he will not bother you again. We must "bind the strongman" (demon spirits) that come against God's people (Mark 3:27). They will resist, and that is where it gets messy! You must be bold and direct; commanding the spirit of darkness to leave.

You have authority; they lost theirs at the Cross! You stand complete in Christ (Col. 2:9-10) and can speak on His behalf. Like a sumo wrestler that cannot be moved, you must stand your ground for Jesus Christ! Victory is yours in the Name of Jesus Christ! Use that wonderful Name in every prayer. The enemy trembles when even the weakest believer turns to God in prayer.

6. Devotional Prayer

This is private, heart-filling prayer. It is spending time alone with Jesus, calling upon His Name, meditating on His Word, yielding our heart to Him. Every pastor wants to develop a praying church, but it starts from the inside out. Private, secret prayer not only grows our inner life, but it will grow healthy churches. During these daily times of private devotion and seeking God, we incorporate the types off prayer mentioned above—praise, adoration, thanksgiving, confession, asking, intercession, and warfare. It is a time to pour out your heart to God and grow in your devotion to Christ.

As He draws near, our heart comes alive. We make sweet resolutions to love, follow, and obey Christ. We yield our spirit to God, and He fills us with His presence. Remember: He loves to hear your voice! Proverbs 15:8 says, *"The prayer of the upright pleases him."*

7. Corporate Prayer

The family that prays together stays together. Corporate prayer is praying with others. It can be in your home as a family or prayer group; it can be in a large setting with hundreds or thousands present. Refreshing, enjoyable, life-giving prayer is coming to a church near you! To pray with others is more than valuable—it is crucial (Acts 2:42 and 3:1).

What Can Hinder Our Prayers?

Many of us approach God on the credit/debit system. If we have been "good" (kind to others, attending church, giving our tithes, performing good deeds), then we expect God to answer our prayers. But if we have not been so "good" (got mad at someone, spoke a bad word, slept in last Sunday, etc.), then we feel rejected by God and unworthy. To base your prayer life on your "track record" is to miss the truth about grace. God loves His kids and will respond when we cry out to Him, even with a "poor track record."

Nevertheless, unconfessed sin hinders our prayers (Isa. 59:1-2). It is important that we draw close to God in prayer...and as we do, we discover there are certain things that will block the answer...

1. Not Spending Time with God

The more time we spend with the Lord Jesus in prayer and study of His Word, the more His presence lingers with us. Fellowship is lingering with God. Do you notice when you fellowship with other believers how hard it is to leave sometimes? You just want to linger with your friends in the presence of Jesus. This is what fellowship with God is—LINGERING WITH HIM. If we ignore our Best Friend, our prayers will be hindered. Read James 4:8.

2. Asking with Wrong Motives

The Lord sees the motives of our heart as we pray. It doesn't make sense to pray with selfishness in our heart. Be careful never to pray out of anger toward another person, or even toward our Lord Jesus. Perhaps you could ask Him to show you in prayer where there are any wrong motives hindering the speedy answer you seek. **Love** is the purest motive that should empower prayer. The more you are hopelessly in love with Him, the more your goals will be lost in His. Read James 4:3, Isaiah 52:11, and Psalm 37:4.

3. Not Asking According to God's Will

How could God give us things He knows would harm us? How could He answer prayers that will distract us from the perfect will of God? Just because YOU think something is God's will does not make it so. Seek first the Kingdom of God, and all the things you ask for will be given to you. The Kingdom of God is the place where God is King, where His will is supreme, where He rules in perfect wisdom. I John 5:14-15, and Matt. 6:33.

4. Doubting That God Will Answer

If we are asking God for something, how silly to ask if we REALLY don't believe He will do it. Never play religious games with God in prayer. Ask Him boldly in faith. Leave your doubts outside when you enter His sanctuary. He has limitless power to do what you are asking Him to do. Just believe! To be double-minded is to pray with doubt in our heart. A single-minded devotion to God will give birth to genuine faith in your heart. Your God is able to do all that we ask or think. It is time to believe for the unbelievable! (James 1:5-8, and Eph. 3:20).

5. *Giving Up Before the Answer Comes*

True faith will not give up when delays come. We must press on in faith and keep asking. It is not a sign of doubt to ask God more than once for the same thing. It is a sign of faith that you know He will come to your side and do the things you request. Hang in there my friend—God is testing your faith with every delay. Often God will test us with delays. He places us in His "waiting room." We pray UNTIL the answer comes. Read Luke 18:1, and Isaiah 62:6-7.

6. *Lack of Unity*

Praying with others increases our effectiveness in prayer. But as we pray, we must be quick to be in true unity and pray in agreement with others. Division among believers diminishes our power in prayer. When we are pulled apart from one another we become dysfunctional. It is next to impossible to pray in power if we are not *one in spirit* with others. Criticism and grumbling will eventually stop the flow of the Holy Spirit and shut down prayer in a church. Instead of holding hands in prayer, try linking hearts—laying down our objections with one another (Matt. 18:19).

7. *Unforgiveness*

Jesus makes it clear that if we hold unforgiveness in our heart, He will withhold from us the things we desire in prayer (Matt. 6:9-15). Release forgiveness, and God will release answers to prayer. Just as YOU need forgiveness daily, so do others. You act the most like Jesus when you forgive like Jesus. True forgiveness is *refusing to be angry again over the wrongs of another.*

Unforgiveness breaks your communication with God. It locks you into the past. Forgiveness will free you in your prayer life and releases the Holy Spirit through your prayers. Empty your heart out to God even about your feelings toward the person who has hurt you. This will help you recognize sinful attitudes that you are not aware of. Helpful Psalms include 52 and 54.

Sometimes it helps to speak to people as if they were there with you. Tell them how you felt when they hurt you. Ask God to forgive them for the specific hurts they inflicted upon you (Job 42:10). Renounce and break any judgments made against the person (Luke 6:37-38). Then, ask God to fully bless those who have hurt you (Rom. 12:14, I Cor. 4:12). It is often appropriate to go to specific people and ask them to forgive you.

8. Prejudice or Hate

Hidden anger in our hearts toward others is a form of hatred. We can never exalt ourselves above others by comparing ourselves with them saying, "I would never do that!" We are predicting our next fall when we speak like that. Let love flourish in your heart, and the God of Mercy will visit you. If you close your heart to others, God will close His heart to your prayers. Prejudice toward another human being, in any form, is sin and will also block your prayers from being answered. (I John 2:9-11).

9. Marriage Difficulties

The most wonderful relationship on earth between a man and a woman is the marriage covenant. If you are married, you must succeed in loving your spouse if you want to succeed in prayer. The God of heaven sees the way you treat your spouse. He will close His ears to you, and your prayers will be hindered if you do not cherish and honor your covenant-partner. Read I Peter 3:7.

Prayer Needs Help to Work.

What are the things that will help us in our prayer life?

◈ **The Bible**—Begin to make your own exploration of the riches of the Scriptures.

◈ **Books on prayer**—The Lord has given us many great books to help us learn. Read some of them.

◈ **Fasting**—Our hunger for God! We fast to be near the Bridegroom/King.

◈ **Community**—Prayerful friendships in the context of a local church and small groups.

◈ **Mentors**—Ask a godly Christian friend to hold you accountable in prayer. Everyone needs a coach, a mentor.

Just Give Me the Basics!

1. *Have your **heart right** with God!* Prayer has no meaning if we don't cleanse our hearts (Ps. 66:18, Isa. 59:1-2).

2. *Have a **thankful heart!*** Unrelenting gratitude for what God has done for you is the secret of a powerful prayer life. King David made many mistakes, but he praised God all the way through his personal "wilder-

ness" until he got to the other side. Come before Him with thanksgiving.

3. *Always admit you are weak!* This is how we grow. God uses our weaknesses as a platform for His strength. It is OK in God's kingdom to be weak; the Lord loves to come and be our strength. He becomes for us our wisdom and our salvation (I Cor. 1:30).

4. *Focus on God's power to meet your need!* That's faith. Just believe that God is able to answer your cry and supply every need you have. **Everything** you need is already yours. Let nothing keep you from prayer. It is your lifeline to heaven. Be addicted to prayer!

Lesson Two

Hearing the Voice of God

❖   ❖   ❖   ❖   ❖

*And the sheep listen to His voice. He calls His own
sheep by name and leads them out. When He has brought
out all His own, He goes on ahead of them, And His
sheep follow Him Because they know His voice.*
John 10:2-4

True Prayer is a love relationship with God—It is
enjoying a relationship, not enduring a religious activity. It
is the privilege of soaring to the very throne of God to
touch His face. It is meeting with God Himself. Our souls
are starved for this sense of awe to speak and to hear from
God. Never forget that Father God loves to share His heart
with His children.

Fellowship with God in prayer is meant to adjust
you, not to adjust God to what you want. We must have
frequent, intimate contact with our Father, our Abba.
Prayer is more than speaking *to* God; it is speaking *with*
Him. You cannot build an intimate relationship on one-
way speeches. As I pray to God, I am aware of this: both of
us speak, and both of us listen.

When we practice two-way prayer, listening carefully and humbly, God often speaks. This prophetic inter-
change is not limited to verbal communication. We can
expect to encounter God in various ways. However we
hear Him, this Divine encounter will always do two things:

it will change us, and we will be given ammunition for spiritual warfare.

As we hear accurately from God, the Church will begin to enter into prophetic praying. Prophetic prayer is praying with revelation and receiving God's response. It is becoming a prayer partner with Jesus. God will not only speak *to* us; He will also pray *through* us.

You must become one who hears from God in the secret closet where you are trusted with strategic prayer assignments. Instead of praying, "Speak Lord; your servant is listening," we most often pray something similar to: "Listen, Lord; your servant is speaking!" Decide today that you will have a heart that will wait on the Lord and listen for His voice.

Your tools for ministry must include a consistent life of hearing from God (Isaiah 50:4-5). Ask Him for the listening ear! Marvelous revelations and a deeper understanding of Scripture await those who ask for it and linger in His presence to hear His voice. Our Lord is known as the great "Revealer of mysteries (Dan. 2:29, 47)." There is much He has to say to the seeking heart.

Sometimes people ask me, "How do I know when it is God speaking? I don't want to be misled. I only want to listen to the Holy Spirit." Here are some simple guidelines for knowing God's voice and discerning when it is the voice of the enemy:

◈ Jesus is a gentle Shepherd; Satan is a condemning and accusing intimidator.

◈ The Lord's voice is often quiet and deeply internal; Satan's is intrusive and vulgar.

◈ The Holy Spirit calls and draws us; Satan threatens, demands, and drives.

◆ Check the content. Does it agree with the Scriptures?

◆ God's voice drips with mercy; He does not condemn our personal worth before Him.

◆ The Lord's voice will change you and touch you.

◆ His voice is rooted in hope, not negativity or despair.

◆ God's Word is for "NOW"; Satan locks us into our past.

◆ God uses the ordinary, not merely the spectacular.

◆ His Word gives more hope, not more condemnation.

◆ God's voice inspires us to love, not to criticize others.

◆ Peace comes from God; anxiety comes from Satan.

◆ The voice of the Spirit always glorifies Jesus as Lord and points us to Him.

How Does God Speak?

We all have a longing to hear God speak to us personally. We would love to have our prayers answered with an audible voice, to know His divine guidance for our days, to hear Him teach us the sacred mysteries. It seems too good to be true. Would the Living God, the Creator of all things actually speaks with me?

The answer is clearly, YES! But there is much we must learn about hearing His voice. We mistakenly think He must speak a certain way; we tend to box Him in to our religious upbringing and narrow expectations. When we become child-like in faith and simply listen, God will speak to us.

1. He Speaks Out of our Intimacy with Him.

Relationship leads to revelation. Intimacy imparts inspiration. It is as we seek His face that direction, guidance, and wisdom will come to us. Why would He want to shout at those He loves? God wants to have our focused, undivided attention so that the mere "look in His eyes" would be enough to know His heart and plan for us. Lord, help us to be as close to you as we can. Help us to look into your eyes for all our needs. See Psalm 27:4-8, and Psalm 32:8-9.

2. He Speaks Any Way He Chooses.

There are countless ways that God can speak to us. So often we miss the voice of the Lord because we presume He can only speak a certain way. It is important to have an ear (heart) that will "listen as one being taught." To be true disciples, we must have an awakened heart, becoming teachable and responsive to what God says.

Your Friend wants to expand your faith to hear Him in new expressions. Although many of the ways God speaks are subjective and must be properly discerned, it is still worth the adventure to have the "listening ear." Read Job 33:14-26, Isaiah 50:4-5, and Hebrews 1:1. We learn from the record of the Bible that God has spoken in the following ways: (This is not an exhaustive list!)

- Dreams
- Pictures in the mind
- Visions

- Parables
- Trances
- By the voice of the Holy Spirit
- Angelic visitations
- Through the Scriptures
- Throne room encounters
- A voice speaking behind us
- Prophetic words
- Words in the night
- Prophetic actions
- Personal inner impressions/burdens
- Through nature
- Signs, wonders, and miracles
- Through everyday circumstances
- Animals speaking
- Face to face
- Through others
- Audible voice
- Still, small voice
- Thundering words
- Riddles or "dark speech"
- Inner voice
- Conviction of sin
- Out of His burning presence (bush of fire)
- Spontaneous ideas and thoughts
- A settled peace
- Prophetic words from gifted ones
- Closed doors/Open doors
- Through the counsel of friends
- Through finances
- Through unanswered prayer

Why not find a quiet spot today and open your heart wide to God. Ask Him to give you specific guidance for the decisions and dilemmas you face. Ask Him to tell you what He thinks of you. Tell Him you want an ear that will listen as one being taught. Begin to praise and worship the Name of Jesus—draw near to Him. Open your Bible to one of the Psalms and read until it touches you.

Now wait in stillness, and then wait some more. Close your eyes. Let the Lord speak to you. Make sure you write down what you hear or what you see. Then respond in humble obedience to whatever He shows you.

Here are some Scriptures that will help you begin your adventure: Psalm 81:13-14; Proverbs 1:23; Proverbs 6:20-23; Matthew 4:4; Acts 8:26,29; 10:3, 18:9-10; Hebrews 3:15; Revelation 3:22; 19:10

3. The Holy Spirit Speaks Through Worship.

Often, the words of a song become the living, speaking voice of the Lord to our hearts. As the Early Church worshipped, God spoke (Acts 13:2). Keep worshipping your King, and it will all make sense to you. Be faithful to spend time in worship at home. Listen to worship music and allow God to soften your spirit to Him. He will speak to you as you worship Him! I cannot tell you how many times the Lord has ministered to me as I pour out my worship to Him. It is out of the place of deepest intimacy that God will speak.

4. Listen for His Voice Through Others.

God has made us dependent upon others to help us grow in Christ. This is why He provides leadership over our lives that will point us to Him. Always listen to your spiritual leaders who speak to you the words of God (Acts 8:30-31). They are sent by the Lord to instruct us and interpret for us the ways of God. Many are the times God's voice can be heard in other people He has sent!

Share your dreams and "words" with others and receive their input. There are no "know-it-alls" in God's Kingdom.

5. God Often Speaks in Pictures, not Just Words.

This is crucial to understand. God's language is parables, pictures, visions, and dreams. God does not just use words in our language to communicate with us (Amos 8:1-2). Be open to learn; this does not come overnight. It will be years before you understand even the fringes of His ways. Keep an open spirit to new ways of listening to the Lord. It is important to open the lens of our heart and receive the revelatory light that God longs to give (Eph. 1:15-18).

6. God Speaks Through Everyday Circumstances.

Be careful not to over-spiritualize how God will speak to you. I once accidentally deleted an email I intended to send—then I understood that my reply would not really be filled with Jesus. God was telling me not to send it. God will speak through just the natural happenstance of our lives. Read Proverbs 1:20-22.

7. Dreams and Visions.

Because dreams and visions are so common among God's people, it is important to address them at this point. Part of the end-time strategy of God is to pour out His Holy Spirit upon His sons and daughters. As a result, they will prophesy, have visions, and dream dreams (Acts 2:17). These dreams will reveal the wisdom and purposes of God for nations, churches, and individuals.

It is crucial for the Church to understand the speaking of the Lord through our dreams. We can expect dreams and visions to multiply and intensify as we approach the return of Christ. Many of God's servants in the Bible were dreamers (Abraham, Jacob, Joseph, David, Daniel, Ezekiel, Mary's husband Joseph, John, Paul). Even ungodly ones received dreams that were from God (Pharaoh, Nebuchadnezzar, Herod, etc.). See Acts 2:17 and I Samuel 3:1-10.

Look at the Benefits of Listening to God.

◈ Supernatural strength – Isaiah 40:31

◈ Direction and guidance – Isaiah 30:21

◈ A manifested sense of His nearness – Psalm 63:6-8

◈ You will have instructions for others – Isaiah 50:4

◈ Courage – Psalm 27:4

◈ Blessing – Isaiah 30:18

◈ Satisfaction – Psalm 63:5

◈ Wisdom – Psalm 90:12

◈ Prosperity – Joshua 1:8, Psalm 1:1-2

Beware of the Two Extremes.

The "God never speaks to me" **or** the "God told me" syndrome! If you are one who is continually saying words like these, it may be time for a minor "tune up."

Those who believe that God never speaks to them often do not have a clue that He has been speaking to them all along—they simply have not detected His voice. Some will actually say, "I *never* dream" or "I *never* hear from God." The Lord DOES speak to reveal Himself; we are just not aware of it (Job 33:14). We are the ones who are often dull of hearing.

The other extreme to avoid is to always be saying,"God told me." This gives the impression that God speaks audibly all the time! The truth is, God does speak to us, but we are often quick to misinterpret what He says because we WANT to hear certain things. Others do not always need to know if the Lord has shown you something. God speaks to us to feed our prayer life, not our egos. The more information He gives us, the more responsible we become to pray and intercede for others. Why not keep it hidden and grow in character?

It is more important that we become like Christ than for others to think we are closer to God than we really are! Never assume you are right about everything you hear. We know only in part (I Cor. 13:9), and, there are times that we are mistaken. We learn that it was not the voice of God, but the voice of our own heart speaking to us.

Wisdom and humility are necessary to discern the true voice of God. If you are having difficulty discerning which voice it might be, you may want to tell the Lord, "I truly want to hear only Your voice. If this is You speaking to me, cause your voice to be even clearer and more urgent. If this is not You, then please cause it to fade." God will bring the answer to this prayer.

> *I have much more to say to you, more than you can now bear. But when He, the Spirit of truth comes, He will guide you into all truth. He will not speak of His own;*

He will speak only what He hears, and He will tell you what is yet to come. He will bring glory to ME.

John 16:12-14

There are many things the Lord wants to speak to your heart, but He will only say them when you are ready to hear. The Lord has commissioned us to hear His voice. Every believer must cultivate the art of listening for the voice of the Lord. The Spirit of truth is not be feared or doubted.

The precious Holy Spirit has a voice. He comes to show us the glories and riches of Christ (Eph. 1:17-18, Col. 2:3). You can trust the Holy Spirit to lead you. His words are more faithful than human teachers (I John 2:20-27).

Biblical Guidelines for Hearing from God

The Bible must be our guide to assure us that it is really God speaking to us. We can trust no other wisdom than the ageless wisdom of the Bible. From Genesis to Revelation we see the God who speaks and desires that all mankind listen. The only valid entry way into the heart of God is the Word of God. Jesus is the Living Word, and the Bible is the written word.

1. Trust the Holy Spirit to Speak to You.

What He has done for others He will do for you! Believe that God will speak to you and wait for Him. Faith opens our ears and keeps us alert to hear His voice (John 10:3). Never compare yourself to others; only wait upon the Lord. Be ready to act on each prayer assignment He gives you. He may cause a person's face to flash before you, or perhaps their name. This is God's way of alerting you to pray for them (Acts 9:10-14).

2. Submit Your Will and Reasoning to the Lord.

When God does speak, it will be awesome—and at times bewildering. Let God stretch you in your understanding. His ways are not your ways. Be prepared for surprises! You may think it was just a silly dream, but it could be God's way of alerting you to pray for someone. God's communication with us is Spirit to spirit. If we analyze everything God says and try to make it fit our "grid" of what God wants or how He would speak, we will miss it. Read I Corinthians 2:9-10.

3. Turn Off Your Own Problems.

A heart filled with anxiety and worry cannot hear from God clearly. Lay aside what troubles you; God is in control (Phil.4:6-7). The biggest problem you could ever have is already solved. You know you will spend eternity with Jesus! At times you may feel troubled about something; that means it is time to pray, not worry! Often, our emotions are no help; They hinder what God wants to say. We can easily be deceived by thinking God's voice is always pleasing to our immediate emotional need, but it is not!

4. Give Your Undivided Attention to God's Word.

Ask God for confirmation from His Word. Most of the time God chooses to speak to you, it will be from an open Bible with a tender heart toward Him. Honor the Word of God, and the Lord will make sure you hear from Him! Sometimes you will feel an intense longing to be alone with God. Yield to that holy impulse and open the Bible, asking the Lord for His prayer assignments for today. It is important that we not just seek a word, but *become a word!* Read Joshua 1:8-9.

5. Write It in a Journal.

Great treasures are found in even ONE word from the Lord. You may not understand what He is saying to you, but you will later. Write it in a journal and watch God open your understanding over time! Many intercessors have found it helpful to keep a prayer journal to record the words God gives you during prayer. God holds these words in high esteem and so should we. When hearing from God, especially in the night, it is important to write the revelation lest you lose it (Hab. 2:2). Others may also profit from what you discover from the Lord.

We wage war with words! Use the Word of God like Jesus did, "It is written" (Matt. 4:4, 7, 10). However, there are also words God gives us that are revealed in prophecy, dreams, and visions. These words, interpreted properly, give us ammunition for our prayer canons (Dan. 7:1)!

6. Wait for the Interpretation.

Even the Lord's prophets in the Bible were often puzzled over what God said to them. Sometimes God speaks of something that will come later; we must be patient and wait for God to make it clear. He always will in time! One day with the Lord is like 1,000 years. He does not live under the constraints of our schedules and ideas. God always moves in the "fullness of time." Receiving revelation from God places us in a position of greater responsibility to walk in wisdom. If you do not understand what God may be saying to you, record it for a later day. See Habakkuk 2:3.

7. Don't Be Afraid of Waiting in Silence.

As the presence of the Lord fills your heart, it is good to quietly wait for Him to speak. Take time to be alone in solitude with God. He loves to see you seek His friendship. For centuries, God's people have found solitude and quietness as a doorway into the Lord's presence. Ask God for wisdom; then wait for it to come. The secrets of meditation are waiting for those who wait. Don't forget Proverbs 8:32-36. We must be those who listen, watch, and wait, for by this we will obtain favor from the Lord. Read Hab. 2:20.

8. Be Prepared to Hear What You Did Not Expect.

The words of God are awesome, incredible—words that release life and power to us. Because God is wise, He will overlook what we WANT to hear and He will tell us what we NEED to hear instead. Just listen and obey all He tells you (Matt. 7:28-29).

Give God your "what ifs" and simply trust and obey. God is all-wise and all-loving. He does not have to explain to you everything He does or everything He tells you. You must be humble and let God lead you. Often, the understanding has to work overtime to catch up with Him (Jer. 18:5-6). Never argue with the wisdom of God!

9. Beware of Setting Time Limits for God to Speak.

It is not wise to set time limits for God. He will disappoint you just to test your faith! It is always best to love God, wait upon Him, and let Him decide what is best for you. You are really blessed if you determine never to be offended by the way God deals with you! People have missed incredible opportunities for God because they had limited the timing for God to move on their behalf. The Lord often waits until we have given up before He moves in power. Read Romans 5:6.

10. Is There a Condition on the Word He Gave?

With most words from God, there is an "IF" clause (II Chron. 7:14). If we pray, God will send revival. If we turn from sin, God will pour out His blessing. If people respond rightly to God, He will change their situations. Be sure to interpret correctly the things God gives.

11. Prove All Things by the Word of God.

The written Scriptures must have the final say in all dreams, visions, and prophetic revelations. So often, our opinions of God's Word keep us from hearing correctly the Word of the Lord. The Lord never contradicts His Word, but He is not afraid to contradict our opinions and traditions regarding His Word. We must seek more light from the Bible to keep us steadfast and fixed on truth. See I Thessalonians 5:19-22.

12. Don't Always Depend on Others to Hear for You.

No one can ever take the place of the Holy Spirit. We must tune our hearts to hear the Lord, not just those who speak for Him. As we go on into Christ-likeness, we must develop a heart that will seek the Lord for ourselves. We want intimacy, not just information. Beware of living off others' faith instead of seeking God's heart for yourself. Read I John 2:27.

13. If Fear Overcomes You, It is the Enemy Speaking.

The sweet voice of the Holy Spirit will not bring ungodly fear into your life. We are to fear, with reverence, the Name of the Lord, but a fear that leads to torment is not from God. Often, we are startled by what He speaks, but this must not be confused with anxious care and fear. God has not given us a "spirit of fear" but a mighty Spirit of power and wisdom (II Tim. 1:7). The voice of Lord will leave us in awe, but also comforted in His grace. There is no accusation in His voice, for even His conviction of sin is what leads us to repentance and cleansing (John 6:20).

14. Distinguish Between Your Thoughts and His Voice.

How easy it is to miss it! As we begin this adventure, there will be many times we step out thinking that God has spoken to us, only to learn later that it was our own heart (or perhaps misinterpreting His word). God's voice has power to change the heart and bless others. Our inner thoughts can be cloudy, confusing, and misleading. Mature friends of God will distinguish between human impressions and God's voice. Read Psalm 29.

15. Have You Done the Last Thing He Told You?

Obedience to all the known will of God is necessary if you are to be one who hears His voice. A willing heart is a hearing heart. Always do the last thing He gave you to do before you seek the next step. As you walk in the light you have, the Lord will give you more light (Ps. 36:9). When our will is yielded to God, we can expect the Holy Spirit to lead us even further. The Lord is patient to wait until our obedience is complete. Read Joshua 1:7.

16. Do Not Always Share Your Revelation.

Wisdom requires that we hold back from telling everything God gives us. Those who consistently hear from God will be quick to veil their knowledge in humility. Most of the time when we blurt out what God is telling us, our motives are mixed with a desire to be seen by others as one who is closer to God than we truly are. Wait until God releases you to share with others your revelation. Paul the apostle waited fourteen years before he shared the experiences God had given to him. See II Corinthians 12:1-10.

17. Try Asking God Questions.

Have you ever thought of simply asking God a question before you go to bed at night? This is one way of receiving incredible wisdom and guidance from God. We must stay in constant communication with the Lord Jesus to make it through the perils of the coming days. By asking direct, clear questions to the Lord in prayer—and by receiving the answers—miracles of power and wisdom will flow.

Jesus said, ASK and it shall be given. He gave no condition or qualification to His statement. We can ask for anything and everything, including answers to questions about the Scripture, our future, decisions in our life, ministry direction—anything! Read Daniel 12:8, Psalm 16:7, 27:4, and Jeremiah 33:3.

Why not ask God your question before you sleep? For those who say God never speaks to them; here is a challenge. For the next seven nights, ask the Lord a specific question and trust the Lord to speak to you in your dreams or upon your bed as you awake in the morning.

Do you need wisdom to make a decision? This is what the great Revealer of Mysteries says: *"If any of you lacks wisdom, he should ask God, who gives generously to all without finding fault, and it will be given to him (James 1:5)."* You must have a question to tap into God's wisdom! This wisdom often comes to us early in the morning (Isa. 50:4). Even Jesus, the greatest prayer example of all, asked questions to learn the wisdom of God (Luke 2:46-47). Often, the disciples of Jesus asked questions of Him (Luke 11:1, Mark 7:17).

"*Great and unsearchable things*" that we have never even dreamed of await us if we simply ask. Let us call upon Him and pray! We are told throughout the Scriptures to "*meditate*" upon the Word of God (Psalm 1:2, Josh.1:8). Meditation leads to inquiry. It is time to gaze upon the beauty of the Lord and to "*inquire in His Temple!*" King David was one who frequently meditated on the goodness of the Lord and awoke in God's presence (Ps. 139:17-18). The thoughts of God are accessible to us even as we sleep. The adventures of the night are ahead for you! Dedicate both evening and morning to hearing from God (Ps. 119:147-148). Fresh revelation is yours for the asking, so gather your morning manna.

"*On my bed I remember you; I think of You through the watches of the night*" Psalm 63:6.

> As you were lying there, O king, your mind turned to things to come, and the revealer of mysteries showed you what is going to happen...The king said to Daniel, "Surely your God is the God of gods and the Lord of kings and a Revealer of mysteries, for you were able to reveal this mystery."
>
> Daniel 2:29, 47

18. Avoid the four Pitfalls.

a. Pride—validating your gift by telling others all you see.
b. Presumption—we do miss it, don't we?
c. Missing God's timing—Father knows best. He will do it.
d. Bringing confusion to others—some are not ready.

What Do We Do with What We Hear?

The Lord has chosen to partner with us so that together we can enter into the fulfillment of the purposes of heaven on earth. There is a longing in the Father's heart to communicate this burden with His prayer partners, called intercessors. There are specific prayers that need to be prayed, and He will help us pray them. But first, we must hear His voice and understand His heart. This is why hearing from God is crucial for end-time prayer ministry to be fruitful. We must hear from the Father and pray His will be DONE on earth as it is in heaven.

As you advance in prayer, you will begin to discern other means that God uses to share His burdens with us. Oftentimes, a strange heaviness will come upon you as the Lord's way of telling you that its time to PRAY. This is not the devil, nor is it a form of depression. It is the Lord's Spirit stirring you to seek His face and discover His prayer assignment (Ps. 27:8).

This is what it means to take the yoke of Christ. As His prayer partners, we willingly take upon our hearts the desire to pray until the burden lifts (Matt. 11:28-30). At other times a weeping will come upon you for no known reason. Again, this is not depression or self-centeredness. It is the Lord's Spirit touching your heart to intercede for another. If you ask Him for specifics, you may see a picture of someone or something flash before your mind that may provide the answer for your question (Acts 9:10-14).

Every prophetic insight we receive is to lead us into intercession. At times it will be to avert evil, and at other times, it will be to release fulfillment of divine promises. Inquire of the Lord when He speaks to you. Ask Him for clarity and for wisdom to know what the Lord wants you to do with what He is telling you.

Remember the words of Samuel: "Speak, Lord, for your servant is listening" (I Sam. 3:10). Become one who waits daily at the Lord's doorposts, awaiting your prayer assignments, and become a prayer partner with the Son of God! **"Blessed is the man who listens to Me, watching daily at my doors, waiting at my doorway" (Prov. 8:34).**

There may be great consequences for NOT hearing God. Israel refused to give heed to the Word spoken from the Mountain of His Presence. Repeatedly we are warned from Scripture to listen and obey the voice of God when He speaks. Ask Jonah!

We must become those who wage war with the prophetic promises that are given. Through them we are able to fight the good fight of faith (I Tim. 1:18-19). Promises from God are "prayer ammo" as we intercede in partnership with heaven. We must not become those who "suffer shipwreck" in regard to their faith by either ignoring the prophetic messages He gives us or by basing our Christian walk on prophetic words alone.

We must war with both the written Word (*"logos"*) and the revelatory word (*"rhema"*). This becomes the sharp two-edged sword of the Spirit for every battle (Eph. 6:17).

The prophet Daniel took a prophetic word that was written by Jeremiah and prayed it through until an angel appeared (Dan. 9:2, Jer. 29:10). He knew the prophetic destiny for Israel was to be brought back out of their Babylonian captivity into their land. Daniel did not just read this prophecy and say, "O, that will be nice." He interceded with all his heart.

"So I turned to the Lord God and pleaded with him in prayer and petition, in fasting, and in sackcloth and ashes."

Daniel 9:3

God's prophet stood in the gap between the help-less condition of his nation and the hope-filled promise of God. This is how we must use every prophetic insight. Now let's learn about intercessory prayer.

"For God does speak—

Now one way, now another—

Though man may not perceive it."

Job 33:14

My Personal Journal of the Things God Has Spoken in Dreams and Times of Meditation

_____

_____

_____

_____

_____

_____

_____

_____

_____

_____

_____

_____

_____

_____

_____

_____

_____

_____

_____

_____

_____

_____

_____

_____

Intercessory Prayer

❖   ❖   ❖   ❖   ❖

Therefore He is able to save completely those who
come to God through Him [you and I] because
He always lives to intercede for them.
Hebrews 7:25

How could we speak of intercession without seeing Jesus, Our Magnificent Intercessor! The subject of intercession brings us to the glorious example of God's Son, our Mediator. Every one of us needs an intercessor, someone to come to God on our behalf (Job 9:32-33). God Himself saw that that we had no one to intercede, so He supplied the need by sending us His Son!

Prayer is the most important part of the present ministry of our risen Lord. Christ's ministry did not end with His death. When He was raised in the power of resurrection, He entered another ministry for us—the ministry of intercession. This prayer ministry of Jesus goes on even while you are reading this page: *"He always lives to intercede for them [us]."*

The God-Man is found before the Father in prayer for His friends, you and me. To find Jesus is to find Him in prayer and through prayer. To really know the Man Christ Jesus is to know an Intercessor. His full life and His full love are given over to prayer as He is surrounded by the Father's glory. More than anyone else, we love Him because He ever lives to intercede for us.

Can you imagine what Jesus is asking the Father to do for you today? It is by His prayers that we are being saved from sin and self and Satan. Will you partner with Him and yield to God—becoming an answer to the prayers of the Son of God? Jesus Christ wants to give you His golden voice of prayer. Jesus actually invites you to join in His prayer time with the Father.

Our Lord Jesus is occupied with praying for you! This is His primary task as He dwells at the Father's right hand. He does not primarily live to judge, to demonstrate power, to command angels. His special Divine vocation is to INTERCEDE for His people.

The Holy Spirit also is engaged in this strategy of advancing the Church. The Holy Spirit is the One who calls you to be a partner in God's end-time plan of intercession. The Holy Spirit is so concerned that you become a prayer warrior and intercessory partner with Jesus that He intercedes for you with Divine groaning too deep for human words (Rom. 8:26).

To become an intercessor is to become Christ-like in your inner man. We enter into fellowship with Him when we become an intercessor. This is your true ministry before God. It is so wonderful to be a prayer partner with Jesus! We can all have a part in this—even if we cannot attend a prayer meeting. You can become a "walking prayer meeting" as you intercede through the day. Busy moms, hurried men, students, and ministers alike—we can all mingle prayers with our daily work. An intercessor is one who maintains a spirit of constant prayer. Here is what the Bible teaches about an intercessor:

Intercessors Are Priests.

It is the work of a priest to worship and intercede before God. The Old Testament priest was one who represented the people before God. He was to carry the burdens of the people into the presence of the Lord. The High Priest carried the twelve tribes over his heart (breast) in the form of a special breastplate embedded with twelve precious stones. The apostle John wrote in Revelation 21 that he saw the Bridal City, the New Jerusalem with these twelve jewels as gates (entryways). A miniature New Jerusalem was carried over the heart of the Priest as he ministered before God.

Today, every believer is called a priest (Rev. 1:6, I Pet. 2:5, 9). All of us have the privilege of bringing the burdens of others before the Lord in prayer. We become a "go-between," bringing the burdens of others to God. This type of prayer is called intercession.

We are called to step in the gap between a hidden God and a helpless person, taking the place of Christ in praying for others. Intercessory prayer is tasting God's love and experiencing how Jesus feels for us. What a privilege we have! This is not for the few but for all. No one could say that this is a standard of prayer that is too high or unattainable. As His priest, your true ministry is before the throne before God, not merely on earth before men. Likewise, every church is called to be an interceding church and must actively pursue this priestly ministry of intercession. It is part of our job description.

The priests in Exodus 30 were given the responsibility of burning incense upon the altar at least twice daily—in the morning and in the evening. This activity was to be a perpetual ministry throughout all generations (Lev. 6:13).

As New Covenant priests, we must be faithful to keep the fires of intercession burning continually upon the altar. It is not to go out! Fervent, continual intercession rises like incense before the Father's throne and moves His heart to respond to our cry. These prayers fill up the golden bowls of incense in the presence of the Lamb (Rev. 5:8). As God's priests worship the Lamb in the beauty of His holiness, we will be empowered to cry out DAY AND NIGHT for God's glory to fall upon His people. Arise, O priests of God! Keep the fires of intercession burning! (Later in this book we will discuss the role of intercessors as watchmen who keep watch night and day.)

Intercessors Are Bridge-Builders.

Your prayers actually build a bridge to bring others back to God. An intercessor "stands in the gap" for others. The gap is the distance between where the person/situation is and where God desires them to be. Between the need we see and the provision we long for, there is a gap that must be filled by an intercessor (a go-between). Every Christian is to battle in prayer for those around us in need (Ezekiel 22:30).

It is time for us to become our brother's keeper by intercessory prayer motivated by love. We step into the breach for others, making our prayers a bridge for them to come to God. People everywhere are falling in love with prayer and intercession. Now is the time for the church to arise with new anointing to build bridges for the lost and wandering ones to return to God.

Listen to these words taken from the oldest book in the Bible, the book of Job:

> *A man may be chastened on a bed of pain with constant distress in his bones.... His soul draws near to the pit, and his life to the messengers of death. Yet if there is an angel* [Hebrews "messenger"] *on his side as a mediator* [Hebrews **"intercessor"**], *one out of a thousand, to tell a man what is right for him, to be gracious to him*

and say [to God], *"Spare him from going down to the pit; I have found a ransom for him* [the blood of Jesus]".... *He prays to God and finds favor with Him,* **he sees God's face** *and shouts for joy; he* [the one on a bed of pain] *is restored by God to his righteous state.*
Job 33:19-26

Here are some powerful truths about intercession we can learn from this passage:

◈ Intercessors are like angels (messengers) from God to intervene on behalf of hurting people.

◈ Intercessors have authority through prayer to heal even those chastened by God.

◈ A true intercessor is a mediator, a "go-between."

◈ Intercessors are precious and rare,*"one out of a thousand."*

◈ Intercessors go to God on the basis of the ransom price of the blood.

◈ Intercessors find favor with God.

◈ Intercessors pray until they see God's face (the answer they seek) and are released with joy.

◈ Intercession will restore fallen ones back to their righteous state.

Fervent intercession contains the power to transform and release people. Earnest intercession makes the believer a king, investing him or her with authority so great that captives may be freed, and prison doors opened (Isa.61:1). We must persist in prayer with bold-ness, using the Name of Jesus and the Word of God until Satan gives up his booty. Our willingness to engage in this type of prayer will decide the eternal destiny of neighbors, friends, coworkers, family, even nations.

Whoever is not loosed from Satan's grip in this lifetime will come under Satan's dominion for eternity. Our prayers hold the great potential for their release. Our prayers can do anything our God can do!

The greatest thing you can do for God and for man is to pray. God shapes the world through prayer. Our intercession paints a target on those who are in need of the gospel. God can then "zero in" on their hearts. He sets His sights on them and strikes them with the arrows of conviction. What goes up will come down! Prayer can turn a heart to God.

Intercessors Intervene on Behalf of Others.

Intercession requires that we identify with the per-son and take upon yourself the entire situation of that per-son you are praying for. We may weep with those who weep and then rejoice with those who rejoice (Rom. 12:15). When we carry another's burdens, we fulfill the law of Christ (Gal. 6:2). Intercession cannot be made without pay-ing some kind of sacrifice on behalf of another.

Jesus paid the ultimate sacrifice for us, and He there-fore has authority to intercede. Intercession and sacrifice are linked. The most powerful, effective intercession is that which costs you something. Your sacrifice of time and emo-tional energy will not be forgotten as you build a wall of protection or favor around those you intercede for.

Who will cry out for this generation? Who will be those who intercede for our children? Listen to the plea of Jeremiah...

"Arise, cry out in the night, as the watches of the night begin; pour out your heart like water in the presence of the Lord. Lift your hands to Him for the lives of your children who faint from hunger at the head of every street" Lamemtations 2:19.

When the people are willing to pay a price in order to be heard, the heart of God is moved. Paul was willing to be eternally condemned if it would mean the salvation of his race, Israel (Rom. 9:3). This willingness and sacrifice of Paul gave his intercession power before the throne. This is the very heart of Jesus that Paul is expressing.

When our intercession takes on that intensity, heaven will be moved on the behalf of others. Both Moses and Paul were great intercessors who led God's people into the Promised Land of their inheritance. These warrior-watchmen carry great authority with God and ultimately transform the lives of people (Ex. 32).

The day will come in the Church that we will begin to support full-time intercessors. Their ministry will be that of a priest bringing the needs of the people before God night and day. The Biblical authority for this is in Genesis. Abraham paid tithes to an Intercessor named Melchizedek.

As this "Melchizedek priesthood" is re-established on earth, the Body of Christ will properly esteem this function of intercessors. Together with worshippers they will be supported by the church to keep altar fires burning before the Lord! The Tabernacle of David will one day be restored with night and day intercession (Amos 9:11-12, Acts 15:14-15).

Intercessors Have Authority to Avert Judgment.

There are times an intercessor will be called to build up a wall of prayer not to keep the enemy out, but to fend off the wrath of God. The awesome power of intercession is that it holds back destruction and wrath and brings instead repentance and revival. Listen to God's heart:

> *I looked for a man* [or a woman] *among them who would build up the wall and stand before me in the gap on behalf of the land so I would not have to destroy it, but I found none. So I will pour out my wrath on them and consume them with my fiery anger, bringing down on their own heads all they have done, declares the Sovereign Lord.*
>
> Ezekiel 22:30-31

God is searching for a man, a woman—one person—who will turn the tide and shape history. We come between God and His people pleading for mercy. This is good news! He is pleading for someone to come and persuade Him *not* to pour out His indignation! The Ancient of Days invites our intercession. This holy argument with God can avert or postpone the judgment due. Our intercession can be used to cut short, lessen, or delay righteous judgment until another day.

So the intercessor becomes one who stands in the gap between God's righteous judgments and the need of the people for mercy. God is earnestly searching for willing intercessors to come before Him to turn back His hand of judgment and destruction. Intercessors must tap into the mercy of God!

Abraham was an intercessor. He prayed on behalf of Sodom. His intercession gave Lot and his family the opportunity to be taken out of the city before it was consumed. The issue of this narrative in Genesis 18 is whether God would spare the whole city if enough righteous people could be found. From fifty to forty to thirty to twenty, Abraham's last plea is, "If there are ten righteous found in the city would you not spare it, Lord?" God agrees with those terms. *"For the sake of ten, I will not destroy it" (Gen. 18:32).*

God quits when man quits. He partners with man in prayer. However, not even ten righteous were found, and in the end, Sodom and Gomorrah were destroyed. God's heart went out to find a solution, an intercessor that would plead their case before Him. Think about it! A single person could avert judgment for a city or a nation if he or she stands before God as an intercessor (I Chron. 21:16). Intercession is the most powerful ministry on earth today. The capabilities of intercession are mind-boggling! Prayer determines destiny!

Moses was a true intercessor. He prayed for his people when they were in great crisis because of their sins. "So He [God] said He would destroy them—had not Moses, His chosen one, stood in the breach before Him to keep His wrath from destroying them" (Psalm 106:23). Moses would not budge; he insisted that God show mercy. Moses became a wall of protection against the wrath of the Lord.

Jeremiah, Jonah, Ezekiel, and the prophets were all intercessors who intervened on behalf of the guilty, sparing entire nations from coming judgment. How America needs prophetic intercessors! God is setting His mark upon the foreheads of His true intercessors who "grieve and lament over all the detestable things" that are done in our land.

Esther was a bold intercessor. At the risk of her life she came before the king and pleaded for her people. With fasting and prayer Esther stood in the gap and won their deliverance. She used her position and privilege to spare the lives of others. This one woman changed the course of history for the Jewish people. She becomes a model, a picture of how intercessory prayer averts judgment and releases mercy. May the "Esther Company" of praying women arise to turn our nation back to God and spare us from coming judgments!

Amos was a prophetic intercessor. He was faithful to insist on mercy. He prayed that God would turn judgment away from the land and God yielded to his plea. Through visionary revelation Amos saw coming devastation and begged the Lord for covering mercy (Amos 7:1-6). Prayer can change the plans of God. Lack of prayer and intercession will lead to judgment. We fill the gap with prayer! There are three basic reasons why God would ever relent from judgment:

◈ Intercessory prayer (Amos 7:1-6).

◈ Repentance of the people (Jer. 18:3-11, Jonah 3:9-10).

◈ The great compassion and mercy of God (Deut. 32:36, Judges 2:18, II Sam. 24:16).

Intercessors Open the Gates of Revival.

Keys to the gates of heaven are given to the intercessors. They have authority to stop hell's worst and release heaven's best. God has given the Church the authority to function in the domain of the Almighty (Matt. 16:19). Intercession takes those God-given keys and uses them to unlock the heavens and release the Holy Spirit. The outpouring of the Spirit at Pentecost was the result of a ten-day intercessory prayer meeting. In Acts 4 the church assembles again for prayer and another power demonstration is poured out. Revival is the result of intercession.

As "holy reminders" we act as God's secretary, telling Him about the appointments He has to keep!

Revival is an appointment with God. We take the promises of an outpouring of the Spirit (Joel 2, Isaiah 64, etc.) and remind the Lord. Every promise of Scripture becomes a point of reminding God to keep His Word. We pray the promises until they are answered. Revival is waiting for "holy reminders" to look into God's Word and tell the Lord it is time to come and keep His appointment with the sons of men. God lets us ask Him to do what He wants to do! May the Lord find a good secretary in YOU that will be faithful to cry out and remind Him to send revival! This is the blessed mystery of becoming a prayer partner with Jesus.

Every move of renewal or revival in church history can be traced back to intercessory prayer. The cry of the Holy Spirit today is, "Lift up your heads; O you gates!" Gates do no not have heads; people do. The gates for revival are men and women who lift up their heads to God and cry aloud for the outpouring of the Spirit. It was not always large numbers of people praying but large prayers prayed by the people. When the Lord looks down on your church, may He never have to say, "Where are my intercessors? Why you have not gone to stand in the gap and call forth for the release of My Spirit? Lift up YOUR heads, O you gates of intercession!"

The gates of revival are the broken-hearted intercessors who have seen the King of Glory and let Him come forth to the earth through their prayers (Ps. 24:7, 9). They are the prayer partners with Jesus who work together for the global harvest. We can never take charge over the Holy Spirit. The wind blows where it chooses. He is the Lord of the Harvest who speaks, and we follow. But the wind of heaven blows wherever there is prayer.

Because Jesus interceded in heaven, the Spirit was poured out. Because we pray on earth, God's Spirit will be at work again. The Church must give herself to believing, persevering, intercessory prayer so that another outpouring of God's Spirit will come, ushering in the great harvest of souls. It is the duty of each of us to cry out for more of God's Spirit (II Chron. 7:14). Even little keys open big doors!

Intercessors Bring in the Harvest with Travail.

"Who has ever heard of such a thing? Who has ever seen such things? Can a country be born in a day or a nation be brought forth in a moment? Yet no sooner is Zion in labor than she gives birth to her children" Isaiah 66:8.

Who is Zion? Many have seen this passage, thinking it referred only to the rebirth of Israel as a nation. This *is* taught here, but *Spiritual Zion* is the Church—Mt. *Zion* (Heb. 12:22-23). It is when Zion, the Church, travails in her barrenness that "she gives birth to her children"!

Intercession opens the way for the Spirit of God to fall upon the lost and bring conviction of sin. If a nation can be born in a day, then our prayers *can* turn a city back to God! God wants *birth* in the church, not converts to our form of Christianity. As a mother travails in labor to give birth, so the Church must travail in intercession for the children to come forth from the nations.

We must accept the divine invitation to participate in the pursuits of God through intercessory prayer. With a holy stubbornness we cannot let Him go until He blesses the nations with His great end-time harvest. Prayer will give the Church the golden sickle with which to harvest. Prayer will release "reaping angels" throughout the earth (Rev. 14:15-16).

The Hebrew word for intercession is *paga* and means "to struggle by prayer, to press forward, to travail, to weep, to come between, to touch, to reach, to strike the mark, to attack, to fall upon." The Scriptures paint a picture of a type of prayer that is…well, messy! You cannot have birth without travail.

Every woman who has given birth to a child knows what travail is. The baby does not birth itself. The Hebrew word for travail is *yalad* which means "the time of delivery or intense labor pains."

For spiritual children to be born, some intercessor somewhere has travailed and prevailed! When the spirit of travail is upon you for the lost nothing else matters. You must labor until birth comes. What grips God's heart begins to grip your heart. It is almost like God desiring an opening for the baby to come forth. Travail creates that opening for new life.

The Church also has the responsibility to travail in prayer for Christians to become mature (Gal. 4:19). No one is born a full grown human, and no one is "born again" a full grown Christian. We all have to grow up spiritually. Paul's burden was that Christ be formed in every believer—until Christ is seen through our personality. Prayer must be with *all* our heart before true transformation comes. We must become God's "holy wrestlers"—**WWF (We Will Fight** until the answer comes!)

We are to intercede and travail for those deceived by legalism, self-righteousness, the control spirit, and false teaching. Our intercession frees others to receive from God. Epaphras did the same thing for the church at Colossae and those in Laodecia and Hieropolis (Col. 4:12-13). The spirit of Epaphras will be restored to the Church. Condemnation will be replaced with fervent, bold, intercession for those among us who are yet to be captured in divine embrace. Those "young sisters/brothers" (Song of Songs 8:8-9) must be nurtured in prayer. If they are built as a wall on the foundation of Christ, we must build for them towers of protection. If they are unstable as a door swinging on a hinge, we must enclose them with fervent intercession.

Our intercessory travail is rooted in the confidence that God is love, and He wants the best for every human being. We must pray to move God's heart. We must appeal to

His heart of love for humanity. Childlike prayer will do this. *Wrestling in prayer* must replace wrestling with each other. The backslidden will return when love moves us to pray. Intercessors must be those who take the young by the hands and teach them to walk. The Lord will turn the hearts of the spiritual fathers and mothers (intercessors) to the children (immature).

Desperate measures must be taken in these desperate days. Have you tried tears? Prayer passion will one day bring us to tears. As the Church enters into the harvest, tears will flow freely. Before we can experience the *public reaping* of a harvest, there must a *public weeping* in our land. Incubated in love, this special gift will be what sets apart the Lord's "reaping angels."

The language of compassionate weeping will never fail to touch the heart. When preaching and singing and testifying falls short, try tears. Men can resist your words, but they cannot resist your tears. Jeremiah was known as the weeping prophet for the many tears he cried over the stubbornness of God's people (Jer. 9:1, Lam. 2:11, 18-19). Paul was one who daily warned the flock of God "night and day with tears" (Acts 20:31).

May the Church find the hidden, weeping prophets that will lead us into end-time glory! From the tearful trenches they will come, bringing their sheaves with them. *"Those who sow in tears will reap with songs of joy. He who goes out weeping, carrying seed to sow, will return with songs of joy, carrying sheaves with him"* (Ps. 126:5-6). There is a holy connection with sowing in tears and reaping the harvest. May we yield our hearts to Him and let Him break us open on behalf of the world.

Intercessors Are Bold Spiritual Pioneers.

It is time to move into the Promised Land of Intercession. Only the bold, the passionate, the pioneers need apply. Effective intercession involves boldness—the confidence of the authority of Jesus rising up in your spirit. Bold prayers will get answers. You need to change your prayer life and tap into *bold praying* (Heb. 4:16). Those who understand they are ONE with Christ pray boldly. There are times for quiet brokenness before God, and there are times of bold interceding before God. The lives of others may depend upon it!

Peter and John were bold when they prayed for the lame man at the Gate Beautiful. Their boldness is what offended the religious spirit of those nearby (Acts 4:13). Spiritual earthquakes will be released when the Church learns to pray with boldness (Acts 4:29-31). Paul asked others to pray for *boldness* to come upon him in his ministry of proclaiming Christ (Eph. 6:18-21).

The Spirit of Discovery must return to the Body of Christ. Paul prayed for this to happen for the believers at Ephesus…"*I keep asking that…the glorious Father may give you the Spirit of Wisdom and REVELATION*" (Eph. 1:17). This Spirit of Discovery will release a fuller knowledge of Christ and His ways into our hearts. When this Spirit touches you, you become a pioneer—a trailblazer for God. New discoveries in God are waiting for you. You *know* there is ground that must be taken for God and that His Spirit is with you to discover it! Like an astronaut for Jesus, you ride the shuttle of prayer to find His end-time purpose and power. Others may not understand what is moving you forward, but onward you must go! May the Spirit of Wisdom and Discovery flood the Church of Jesus Christ in these last days! May wagon trains loaded with passion set out on the course of brave, new discoveries!

Intercessors must be given freedom to push the boundaries and extend the borderlines. It is the work of the devil to make you accept the narrow box he has put you in. It is as though God has given you a million-acre ranch to live on, but the devil wants to limit you to one acre. Praying pioneers will go to the backside of the desert just to see what's there (like Moses). Faith will enable us to see the true borderlines and reach forth with vision to move out and claim what God has given us (Phil. 3:12). It is time to extend our borderlines into the devil's territory and drive the "ites" off the Land.

Bold, strategic breakers will push the lines back to where God has ordained them to be. Those with a fore-runner anointing must move ahead and open the way for the Bride to mature and walk in the fullness of our inheritance! Do not throw off the burden to pray when it comes upon you—be bold to act upon it. Boldness means casting off the accusation of the enemy when you come to God in prayer. *You must* push aside all feelings of inferiority, sin-consciousness, and condemnation as you intercede. This is the enemy's strategy to deflate you and cause to be self-focused. Because of the blood of His Son, God does not even remember what you did wrong.

Get Started in Intercession.

The Lord loves to hear your voice in prayer (Song of Songs 2:14-16). He calls your voice sweet. It touches the Heart of Jesus that a fallen, incomplete believer seeks His face. You cannot pray a "bad" prayer. He filters out our funny vocabulary and clumsy emotions to find our real heart. Come to Jesus in prayer and expect to find a smile, not a frown (James 1:5). Jesus does not find fault in you when you come to Him (Song of Songs 4:7). Start in this place of sweetness and sacred confidence. A prayer life will grow as your capacity to know His love grows. Those most powerful in prayer are those who are ravished by His love. Let every encounter with Jesus in prayer be a sacred time of sharing your heart with Him and listening as He shares with you His secrets. How do we get started in intercession?

◈ Tell Jesus you love Him and then ask Him to help you become a prayer partner with *Him*!

◈ You will prevail in prayer as you personalize the love of God and begin to hunger for Him.

◈ Pursue a regular prayer time. Be ready for new levels of personal discipline.

◈ Be willing to obey instantly as you maintain a clear conscience before God and others.

◈ Get used to feeling your weakness in prayer. The Spirit helps us in our weakness (Rom. 8:26).

United We Stand

❖   ❖   ❖   ❖   ❖

How good and pleasant it is When brothers live together in unity! It is like precious oil poured on the head...Running down on Aaron's beard, Down upon the collar of his robes. It is as if the dew of Hermon were falling on Mount Zion. For there the LORD bestows his blessing, Even life forevermore.
Psalm 133

There is something powerful that takes place when believers come together to pray. As we join our hearts with others at the throne of grace (Heb.4:16), we can expect even greater impact. Prayer is more than our private devotional time with God; it is meant to be a shared experience with others in a corporate setting. The Lord loves to see His kids praying together with passion and with unity. You and I are called to be prayer pioneers.

The early disciples gathered together out of their devotion to prayer (Acts 2:42). Corporate intercession was the consistent practice of the Early Church, providing the fuel for revival and miracles. Every church that is pursuing the heart of God must establish regular, corporate times of intercession. These united prayer gatherings will one day become 24-hour prayer centers for every region of the earth as God re-establishes the "Tabernacle of David" among the nations.

Look at what God says about His end-time intercessors: *"These I will bring to my holy mountain and give* them joy in my house of prayer. Their burnt offerings and sac-rifices will be accepted on my altar; for my house will be called a house of prayer for all nations" (Isaiah 56:7).

The Lord longs to bring joy into His house of prayer. Enjoyable prayer is about to be released into the prayer rooms across the earth! His promise is that HE will give those who are dedicated to prayer great joy. His lovesick worshippers will fill the House of Prayer as He makes it enjoyable to spend time with Him.

Heaven Waits for Earth!

Heaven waits for earth. The move of God must come to the earth by aggressive, even furious prayer. The move in heaven is controlled by the move on earth. Listen to what Jesus has taught us: *"Whatever you bind ON EARTH will be bound in heaven, and whatever you LOOSE ON EARTH will be loosed in heaven"* (Matt. 18:18).

This is in the context of united, believing prayer. There must be a move on earth before there is a move in heaven. We are given the keys and must utilize them before heaven moves! It is not heaven that binds first, or looses first; it is earth. Our prayers must bind everything that is contrary to heaven and loose everything that God wants to be done on earth. The Sovereign Lord wants the Church to control heaven!

Can you see this? There is a power that God puts under the control of His interceding people. Just as Moses' uplifted hand controlled the outcome of the battle (Ex. 17:9-11), so intercessors are those who lift their hands on earth that heaven's grace will pour forth on earth's battlefields. Truly, God wants us to *win* and taste *victory*, but if we do not pray aggressively, battles may be lost. God will actually yield to our plea! Our Father lets His sons "pin Him to the mat" by intercession.

*"This is what the Sovereign Lord says: Once again **I will yield** to the plea of the house of Israel and do this for them"* (Ezek. 36:37).

United Prayer and the Power of God

Jesus taught His disciples that the power of prayer is multiplied when believers come together to intercede. One can chase a thousand and two can chase ten thousand! Using the mathematics of heaven, only seven praying in one accord could chase one billion! World changing prayer will result when we agree with others and pray in unity. This is why Jesus always sent out His disciples two by two.

To pray together in one spirit with one heart is to touch heaven. There is a corporate model of prayer in the Bible that is not individualistic. Our goal must be to experience the blessing of Psalm 133, which requires true unity:

*"I tell you that **if two** of you on earth agree about anything you ask for, it will be done for you by my Father in heaven. For where **two or three come together** in My name, there am I with them"* (Matthew 18:19-20).

*"This is the confidence **we** have in approaching God: that if **we** ask anything according to His will, He hears us. And if **we** know that He hears **us,** whatever **we** ask—**we** know that **we** have what **we** asked of Him"* (I John 5:14-15).

*"They **all** joined together constantly in prayer"* (Acts 1:14).

*"When the day of Pentecost came, they were **all together in one place** [praying]"* (Acts 2:1).

"After they prayed, the place where they were meeting was shaken. And they were all filled with the Holy Spirit and spoke the word of God boldly. All the believers were one in heart and mind" (Acts 4:31-32).

The longing of Jesus was that all His followers would be one in spirit and in glory with Himself. There is a sense in which every time we come together as one to intercede, we are bringing delight to the heart of the Lord Jesus—and in part, answering this prayer.

Corporate prayer meetings are a kind of practice for heaven's glory! Praying together releases heaven on earth and takes us into our destiny. There is a measure of God's Spirit that will not be given to the Church until we come together in united, sustained prayer. God's power cannot exceed the united prayer of the Church.

There is an interesting dynamic that takes place in the corporate setting. People coming into the prayer room or meeting place focus on God and engage their spirits at the deepest level. Our attention span tends to be longer when we pray together. We tend to be able to pray longer when we pray together. People really do come alive when God's Spirit is moving in the time of prayer.

Two are better than one; they can chase ten thousand distractions away. When hundreds or even thousands gather for intercession, power is released. We are enabled to aggressively engage with God rather than passively disengage while others are praying. It becomes a holy peer pressure for all of us to stay united in the spirit. Those weak in prayer are taught; those strong in prayer are able to lead and encourage without undue coaxing. The commanded blessing is found when we all gird our hearts for action and come together as one. Something happens when churches pray!

How to Have a Great Prayer Meeting

There is an etiquette that is proper when we come together to have a corporate prayer meeting. You may pray any way you like at home, but in a corporate gathering there are some things that release or quench the Holy Spirit in our midst. Many give up on going to prayer meetings because they are boring and become easily distracted.

There really is no *one* model to follow for prayer. Scriptures give us many models and strategies. Some pray loudly, others softly or silently. Some prayer groups all pray at once; others pray one at a time. The Creator will perhaps give birth to many more new models of intercession before the return of our Lord Jesus. The following are merely observations over the years that seem to help keep life in a corporate prayer setting.

1. The Proper Focus

True prayer must be addressed to our heavenly Father. There are about forty New Testament prayers recorded in the Scripture; all are addressed to God. We have no New Testament prayer directed at the devil. Jesus clearly taught us to pray to the Father (Matt. 18:19, Luke 11:2, 11:13). The prayer of Jesus in John 17 was directed to the Father. Even in the warfare epistle of Ephesians, the apostle Paul prays to the *"Father of Glory"* (Eph. 1:16-17). The prayer focus of the book of Revelation is to Him who sits on the throne (the Father) and the Lamb (the Son) (Rev. 4).

True prayer is focused on the throne room. If our focus remains on the throne room of eternity, it will free us from "preaching prayers." These are exhortations and descriptions of events rather than true petitions to God. Many corporate prayer meetings are stifled by "preaching prayers" that inform rather than powerful prayers that plead with God. Prayer must always be for an audience of One. Exhortation should not be done in prayer. The more we fill our hearts with the throne vision of

Ezekiel 1, Revelation 4-5, and John 17 the better and more potent will be our times of prayer! When the heavens open, you will see a *throne*.

We become prophetically alert in the Holy Spirit when our focus is on the throne room, not the prayer room, who is praying, how they are praying, etc. We are able to discern the "air currents" of the Holy Spirit and echo the heart of God through our prayers. Higher levels of His glorious presence are released through united, focused prayer.

True prayer maintains a positive focus. For faith to operate, we must pray with gratitude and confidence. Our times of prayer are spent praying for a release of the Holy Spirit, for righteousness to prevail, for grace to empower, and mercy to triumph. It is more important to ask God for the impartation of good instead of a negative focus on removing evil. Good overcomes evil. This focus enables us to pray in the love of God for the ones in darkness. It also provides "shock absorbers" for a prayer meeting when another intercessor prays differently than we do. Grace-centered prayers touch in agreement with the throne of grace.

"Let the word of Christ dwell in you richly as you teach and admonish one another with all wisdom, and as you sing psalms, hymns and spiritual songs with gratitude in your hearts to the Lord" (Col. 3:16).

Paul prays for weak, immature churches and begins his prayers with thankfulness and gratitude for their budding virtues (I Corinthians 1). Many of us do not even realize how negative and non-biblical our praying has become. To praise the Lord in the midst of our fallen condition glorifies His Name. To pray with this positive focus frees our heart to carry the burdens of the Lord in this age. When the majority of the people in a prayer meeting pray with their eyes on the throne and a positive focus and renewed mind,the results will be staggering. We will begin to enjoy prayer with this focus.

A false sense of humility will cause us to dwell always on what is wrong when the Lord commands us to rejoice as we come before eternity's throne. Boldness is not pride; it is the confidence that all our righteousness is in Christ and not ourselves. Pride is the wrong confidence that rests in our experience, gifting, or presumed wisdom. Pride will destroy unity and lead us astray when we come together in prayer.

Humility is responding to God, not just a weak will or quiet temperament. To pray boldly before the throne of grace is the command of Scripture (Heb. 10:19-25). With a positive focus we are enabled to hear from the Lord and dwell on His goodness, not the faults of one praying next to us. If our eyes turn off the Lord, we will invariably become critical of how others are praying, the words they use, problems in their lives, etc. It is impossible to pray if criticism is in the midst of the prayer meeting. If we discern that something is wrong, turn it into prayer not criticism. Let us be those who wear "grace glasses" and see one another with eyes washed with love (Song of Songs 5:12).

True prayer brings a proper joy and gladness into the prayer meeting. The Lord has said He would *make them joyful in My house of prayer" (Isa. 56:7)*. It is a religious spirit that wants to make every prayer meeting into a time of confession and repentance. Introspection apart from genuine conviction of the Holy Spirit moves us away from God's heart, not closer. There is a time to weep and a time to laugh. We are loved greatly by Jesus.

As our Friend and Bridegroom, He encounters us with love and joy. Divine romance needs to be brought into the prayer meeting! We are His Bride and earnestly love Him. How can we be negative when our thoughts are filled with the a book meant to be prayed by the Bride.

True prayer is not just an opportunity to vent our problems or frustrations. The only proper focus of any prayer meeting is the Person and Glory of Jesus Christ. Yielded hearts will make room for Him, even when we are burdened with many cares. Because of our inexperience and insecurities, there remains the danger of witchcraft in the prayer room. Both revival *and* witchcraft are born in the prayer room. We are praying out of order when we pray *our desires* upon someone else.

Our words affect others. This is why praying the Scriptures over others is the most desirable way to insure we are praying God's heart for them. In time, God will trust you with "inside information" to pray for others as you walk with a pure heart. This revelation given to you by the Spirit is *confidential* information and ammunition for your prayer life - not ammunition for your conversation with others. Pray with wisdom and *never* pray confidential information in the company of others!

2. The Proper Atmosphere

Human beings need to feel special, wanted, valued. If possible, make it known that everyone has something to contribute to a prayer meeting and make sure there is ample freedom for people to pray and intercede as God touches them. Some will be noisy; some will be quiet. Some will be bold; some will be broken. Some will pray powerfully, some will pray timidly.

We must give the Holy Spirit freedom to move among His intercessors in whatever way that pleases Him. It is wise for the bold ones to "throttle back" at times to let the timid ones step forward. Coming to a prayer meeting with "shock absorbers" on our heart is needful.

Some will pray differently than you, more loudly than you, longer than you, but determine *before* you come to a prayer meeting that God loves to hear His people pray and *we will too!*

Remember: We come before a throne of grace, not a throne of theological accuracy. None of us have all the truth of God nor are always theologically correct in all we pray. We simply pray out of our hearts to the One who sits on the throne of grace (Heb. 4:16). Intolerance or impatience in the prayer room is a sure way to be offended and be defeated by the enemy from even entering in to the sacred chambers of prayer.

Jesus taught His disciples that it was better to swallow a gnat than to choke on a camel (Matt. 23:24). Gnats are those pesky things about others that "bug" you. Swallowing a few gnats (being patient to endure the ways of others) is much better for your health than choking on a camel of self-righteousness!

It is also vital that you have a regular place of prayer. Perhaps a room in your church or home could be dedicated as a "house of prayer"—a place sanctified for sacred communion with God. It is equally important to bring into your prayer meeting a spirit of worship. It is often best to have instruments accompany the prayer times, aiding and strengthening the spirit of supplication in the room.

This is the glorious ministry of the harp and bowl (Rev. 5:8). God's worshipping people in heaven have in one hand a harp (worship) and in the other hand a golden bowl of incense (the prayers of the saints). There is over your city a golden bowl that must be filled with the prayers of God's united people crying out for revival.

The eternal Bride ministers to Christ in this way—may it be done on earth as it is in heaven! As we gather to prayer, it is proper to bring both worship and intercession before His throne.

Don't forget worship. It becomes a booster rocket for the prayer meeting. We have seen many cold, formal prayer meetings come to life through worship. Perhaps you could play soft worship songs in the background to "paint a canvas" for the prayers of the saints. The highest form of intercession is worship—and the privilege of worship is intercession.

3. The Proper Leadership

Have someone with leadership grace be in charge of the corporate prayer meeting. It is so important that the group understands that there is a brother/sister who is overseeing the meeting and that excesses will be reigned in. Without this confidence, the people will struggle with boundaries and often the most insecure and needy will dominate. When there is something that may need a mild correction, it is best to simply wait until after the meeting and explain the protocol to those who may need help.

If it is a major distraction taking place, often simply placing your hand on the shoulder of the person indicates you may want to add something or steer the meeting another direction. May we always be those gracious, gentle shepherds who give the flock of God the freedom they need to pour out their hearts before God. Many times what seems like a distraction is truly the heart of God coming forth from one of His lambs.

Never give a public correction unless it is obvious to all that the Holy Spirit has been grieved. Wise leaders have grace to correct without even the most sensitive being harmed. Let us ask for that grace to be ours (II Tim. 2:24-26).

4. The Proper Freedom

There are times when God pours out the Spirit of supplication (Zech. 12:10) that the prayer meeting looks more like the birthing room than anything else. An intercessor in travail may experience pain for others, groaning on their behalf.

This is why intercession is not so quiet at times. Eternal purpose is being birthed on earth. Intercessory prayer meetings are the womb of the Church. The spiritual midwives (intercessors) are birthing God's purpose. The more intense the labor, the closer is the time of birth. Many churches do not understand this and want to silence the groans of labor pains. This very travail will bring in the harvest. It is best to instruct those new to intercessory prayer what is happening. (Beware of those who simply make noise or have their own emotional brokenness and mistake that for true intercessory travail).

The hope of the world is an intercessory army arising to take her place as the warring bride (Eph. 5-6), armed with the dangerous weapons of the promises of God. When Zion travails, she brings forth her children! At times it is best to wait and see what God is bringing forth when someone expresses themselves in ways you are not used to—you may be in the midst of pre-revival travail!

A word must be given in regard to freedom in prayer. Like every other aspect of our lives, personal freedom will often be laid aside in order to achieve a common purpose and unity. We defer and yield to one another, for this is the way of Christ. Inappropriate pursuit of expressing our freedom may bring personal edification, but it often quenches the Spirit in a prayer meeting. It is always best to flow together as one, and not use our liberty as an opportunity to show off a gift or display our freedom.

5. *The Proper Models:* The Lord's Prayer

"One day Jesus was praying in a certain place. When he fin-ished, one of his disciples said to him, 'Lord, teach us to pray, just as John taught his disciples'" Luke 11:1.

The prayers of Jesus were so powerful even to the disciples, that they pleaded with Him to teach them His secret. Jesus was the Teacher of Prayer. We notice two things here: (1) Effective prayer can be learned; (2) The most effective environment for learning about prayer is in the context of discipleship (a mentoring relationship). John taught his disciples, and Jesus teaches His followers by example. Do you want to learn to pray? Desire is the first step: "Lord, teach me to pray!"

Students of the Bible throughout the ages have concluded that one of the greatest prayer models of all time has been given to us by our Lord Jesus in what is known as the "Lord's Prayer" (Matt. 6:9-13). In just 68 English words, Jesus models for us how to pray. As a young boy, I was taken to a church where this was prayed in unison every Sunday morning. I could even recite it from memory. For years after I experienced the new birth, I did not pray according to this model, feeling it had been over done. But now I have learned that it con-tains the wisdom of Christ that can be utilized in your corporate (and devotional) prayer times.

Within the Lord's Prayer are all the elements of our devotional life in God and a progression of moving within the veil. Notice the scope of this prayer:

◈ **Worship**– Our Father… hallowed be Your name.

◈ **Intercession**–Your Kingdom come, Your will be done.

◈ **Personal Petition** – Give us this day our daily bread.

◈ **Confession** – Forgive us our debts.

◈ **Forgiveness** of others – As we forgive our debtors.

◈ **Guidance** – Do not lead us into temptation.

◈ **Warfare** – Deliver us from evil.

◈ **Bold Declaration** – Yours is the Kingdom. . . .

It is not necessary to pray exactly what is written, nor does it need to be prayed by everyone in unison. However, the Lord's Prayer is a proven pattern to be used as a springboard to launch into intercession. The end-time Church will use this as a Biblical outline for corporate prayer. If you are having intercessory prayer meetings that are 'stuck in a rut' try praying this model. Notice it begins and ends with a praise focus on God and His glory:

"This, then, is how you should pray: Our Father..."

Our confidence in prayer is established upon our security and love from a Father. We rejoice in the privileges of being His beloved ones, His favorite ones in all the earth. It is our great privilege and joy to call Him Father. The Father's love and acceptance are always real, even when we don't feel it. We approach Him in fellowship with others, for He is *our* Father. This is corporate intercession over our birthright as His children. We are the "church of the firstborn" (Heb. 12:23) and therefore have the rights of the firstborn. Our full inheritance as His firstborn sons and daughters is to be prayed down as we look to **"Our Father."**

"in heaven..."

Enthroned with Jesus, our calling is heavenward (Phil. 3:14, Col. 3:1-3). Every time we pray our desires and longings must turn to the dwelling place of the Lord. We find our heart's true home in the place of prayer. Notice the heavenly gaze of David: *"One thing I ask of the Lord, this is what I seek: that I may dwell in the house of the Lord all the days of my life, to gaze upon the beauty of the Lord and to seek Him in His temple"* (Ps. 27:4). This heavenly attraction must fill our heart in prayer, delivering us from the need to be heard by men. Our cares vanish as we turn our thoughts to the One who is **"in heaven."**

"hallowed be Your name..."

Adored and worshipped is that name! We recognize the virtues and beauty of God as we meditate upon Him. Too often, we come to pray and meditate on ourselves. It is time to make the name of Jesus our meditation. His name reveals His personality. It is delightful to speak of His beauty in prayer. All the names of God reveal what He has promised to be in us. Take one of the many names of God and make them your mediation. Worship is the true way of "hallowing" (adoring) the name of Father God.

"Your kingdom come..."

"Come, Kingdom of God!" This is the cry of God's people in intercession. If we are to pray for the coming of the kingdom, our hearts should be prepared. We must lay down our kingdom to make room for His. With a willing spirit to lay everything aside, praying pioneers will say, "Come, Kingdom of God!"

To say "yes" to this kingdom is to say "yes" to change. We long to be under the lordship of Jesus, our King. We not only pray that His kingdom come, but we pray for grace to be transformed into a worthy subject of that kingdom. We can say to our King, "Reign over me and all that is around me. I accept Your rule and will obey You." When we gather for corporate intercession, it is right to pray that His kingdom comes to our hearts, our homes, our churches, and to the nations of the earth. May we all lift one voice as we pray, **"Your kingdom come."**

"Your will be done..."

This is the longing of our hearts, to do the will of God. It is important to speak to your needs and say, "Be done, will of God! Be done in my family, my church, and my workplace." Proclaim the right of God to enforce His will over you and over every spiritual foe you face. This is a declaration of God's sovereign power to do within us all He longs to do. We were made for His pleasure, not for sin, discouragement, and fear. This prayer is also a prophecy that God will win your battles and release His wisdom to maintain victory in all situations. It is the mighty sword of His Word He has given to you in this prayer. Take authority with these words: **"Your will be done."**

"On earth as it is in heaven..."

Whatever God has in heaven, you can ask for on earth. Holiness, peace, victory, joy, worship divine revelation, power, glory, freedom, and serenity. All of these virtues are filling heaven even as you read this page. Intercession pulls down heaven to the earth. Praying pioneers will storm the citadel of heaven as violent ones who will not take "no" for an answer. We will ascend the hill of the Lord with holy hands raised to Him, asking for the heavenly glory to be *on earth!* There are things you will never experience in God if you do not ask Him. Begin to pray that heaven will touch your earth, for you were made from dust! This is your inheritance in Christ and must be claimed in prayer.

Heaven releases itself on earth when the Church comes together to intercede and *ask.* The standard of the Church must be a heavenly one, not a cultural one. We do not need the ways of men, but the ways of God that are higher than man's ways. We cannot rest, nor give Him rest until what is done in heaven is done on earth. We want heaven's worship, heaven's peace, and heaven's power in the Church. May there be night and day intercession before the throne of God pleading for God to move **"on earth as it is in heaven!"**

"Give us today our daily bread..."

Daily provision of "bread" is our promise in Christ. This is an incentive to pray the promises of God regularly. Take His promises and speak His "amen" over all He has told you He would do. They are all to be fulfilled as we claim them and touch them in prayer. This "bread" includes material provisions, but also the spiritual "bread" that nurtures our life in God: fresh revelation knowledge, healing ("the children's bread," Matt. 15:22-28), power for ministry, gifting, anointing. All these may be received by daily prayer and corporate intercession. The words "Give US" speak again of the community of believers coming together for prayer. Perhaps there is within this verse a hidden prophecy of a time when the Church will once again meet *daily* to ask the Lord, "Give us today our daily bread."

"Forgive us our debts..."

We all have sin in our lives that must be forsaken and purged by the blood of Christ. Daily cleansing in grace is a must for intercessors. This is the priest coming to the laver (washing bowl in the Temple) before coming to the throne. Praying this will force us to "own up" to our humanity and guilt before a holy God.

After praying this and receiving His cleansing forgiveness, we are humbled to receive more understanding as His little children needing help. Further revelation comes by a deeper cleansing from sin. There is always a need in the Church of Jesus Christ to ask for forgiveness as we move into His heart. We know that His willing Spirit will give us the forgiveness we ask for. Identificational repentance is implied by these words, **"Forgive US our debts."**

"As we also have forgiven our debtors..."

Forgive as often as you want to be forgiven – this is the lesson of this prayer. There is nothing as serious as unforgiveness in the heart. It reduces our prayers to hypocrisy. We must press in to the grace of forgiving all that offend and injure us. We must take a pre-determined posture before the world that we will seek to be un-offendable. We decide ahead of time not to be offended by the deeds of others and extend true forgiveness whenever we are mistreated.

This is divine insulation for the heart. The evil cycle of *sin > offense > sin* is broken by an attitude of forgiveness. Curses are shattered, and strongholds demolished when you forgive your debtors. This prayer is corporate (united with others) for it is written, **"as WE also have forgiven OUR debtors."**

"And lead us not into temptation..."

This is a prayer for power to overcome sin and to be freed from the snares of life. There are temptations you may escape if you pray. Intercession builds a wall of protection around your soul. It is taking the armor of God and putting on each piece by prayer. Prayer clothing is God's armor for the soul and will deliver us from temptation. This verse causes us to wonder how many temptations we may not have had to experience in life if we had prayed. Every believer walks in grace, but there is a measure of "saving grace" that comes only when we intercede.

It is impossible to over emphasize prayer to protect you and your loved ones from harm. This prayer is intensified as we come together as one. Churches may pray this with confidence that the health and future of the Church will be preserved through corporate intercession. In these difficult days of world tension and pressure on all sides, it is crucial that the church comes together to say to God our Father, **"and lead us not into temptation."**

"But deliver us from the evil one"

It is clear that *intercession thwarts demonic strategies.* True deliverance from the evil one who walks this earth can only be secured as we intercede with others. "Us" is repeated throughout the Lord's Prayer to show us that it is corporate intercession that is in view. A church that neglects having consistent, regular prayer meetings can expect to be "beat up" by the evil one. It is *prayer* alone that can bring deliverance from the schemes of the enemy.

There is additional help for this kind of prayer found in Psalm 91. It is wise to take this psalm and pray its contents over your church and family. To pray together as a body will increase the hedge-building around your church. No one is wise enough or discerning enough by him or herself to detect every scheme of Satan. We must have corporate prayer. Not a pastor, a prophet, nor an apostle is enough—all of us must pray as one, asking in unity that the favor of God will **"deliver us from the evil one."**

Hints for Your Corporate Prayer Time

1. **Ask for the nations to receive the revelation of salvation.** Our inheritance is to be the conversion of nations, not just our neighborhood (Ps. 2:8, Isa. 55:5). Both Paul and Peter prayed for the understanding of salvation for all men (I Tim. 2:1-8, II Pet. 3:8-9). Place maps, flags, prayer letters, pictures of missionaries, etc. around your prayer room to help you stay focused on the need of the nations.

2. **Come to a prayer meeting ready to pray – enter in!** It is sad how many Christians never pray out loud. If you have difficulty with this, ask a spiritual leader to pray with you that God would empower your heart to speak forth. The bolder you become, the more powerful your prayers will be. Take the weapon of prayer and use it! (Eph. 6:18)

3. **Try to limit "preaching prayers" or using prayer to exhort others.** We come to talk to God, not to man. Our meeting is for an audience of One. There will be other times and places for you to use your exhortation or speaking gift.

4. **Honor the protocol of the meeting.** Every church and prayer meeting is different. We all have different

styles and formats for prayer. It is best to allow the flow of the meeting to be directed by those in charge. If you feel the Lord is giving you a burden, a word, or an impression of something, simply write it down and hand it to the leaders and let them discern the heart of God. It is always best to flow as one spirit and one heart in prayer—how glorious this is!

5. **Believe for things you cannot even imagine, then go further!** Your faith needs stretching. Holy Spirit prayers will go further than your imagination (Eph. 3:18-21). Your prayers should go beyond your thoughts and comprehension. The future belongs to the intercessors who believe the future into being. Through your prayers, an alternative future may happen as you pull the will of God down to the earth.

6. **Develop a culture of spiritual aggression and boldness in the prayer room.** Read Isaiah 64 before a time of corporate intercession. Notice the bold faith to press in for God to "rend the heavens and come down." It is not necessary to scream or shout, but neither is it to be forbidden. God is seeking our sincere passion to awaken His heart. When we grow desperate enough, passionate enough, and prayerful enough, the Lord will answer our cry, and the Church will become His Throne of Grace upon the earth!

7. **Expect great answers.** This is the hour of destiny for planet earth. The Scriptures will soon be fulfilled. May this be the generation of those who seek His face. We have been given privileges that even angels do not have. There is no record of angels praying. *ask, seek and knock!*

"I love you, O LORD, my strength.
The LORD is my rock, my fortress, and my deliverer;
My God is my rock, in whom I take refuge.
He is my shield and the horn of my salvation,
My stronghold.
I call to the LORD, who is worthy of praise,
And I am saved from my enemies."
Psalm 18:1-3

Lesson Five

The Prayer War

❖ ❖ ❖ ❖ ❖

*For though we live in the world, We do not wage war as
the world does. The weapons we fight with are not the
weapons of the world. On the contrary, they have divine
power to demolish strongholds.*
II Corinthians 10:3-5

Prayer *is* spiritual warfare! It is impossible to enter
into the realm of prayer and not be contested. For when
God hears our prayer, Satan's plans are defeated. When
we pray, we are enforcing the laws of God's kingdom in
a fallen world. Prayer brings the intercessor into the heavenly dimensions, where angels and demons struggle to
implement their strategies. Intercessory prayer "tips the
scales" on the side of heaven.

Everyone who learns to pray will sooner or later
become skilled in spiritual warfare. Nothing is more
frightening to the devil than to see a humble Christian on
his knees. Nothing is more powerful in the hands of God
than a broken-hearted intercessor. It is time to inflict
damage on the kingdom of darkness!

Calamities can be prevented when we pray.
Demonic strategies are uncovered and exposed when we
pray. Forces of darkness are opposed and pushed back
when we pray. God's secrets are shared, evil is thwarted,

the power of sin is broken, power is poured out, wisdom imparted, and the kingdom expanded—all of these things take place when we pray! More is done for God on earth by prayer than any other spiritual activity. We must do more than pray, but nothing can be accomplished if we are not a praying people.

Where to Begin

Spiritual warfare boils down to the individual. Each one of us must cast down wicked thoughts, deal with impurity, and declare war on our secret sins. Perhaps the greatest weapon of warfare is repentance. As we come clean and deal with every compromise and pocket of darkness within our hearts, we are prepared to hold the sword and render judgment on the powers of darkness over churches and cities.

Tolerated sin prevents us from ascending the "hill of the Lord" and becoming His instrument of spiritual warfare (Ps. 24:3-4). Prayerfully ask God the difficult question: "Is there anything in my life or any thought I hold in my heart, or any habit in my lifestyle that would quench Your Holy Spirit?" It is absolutely vital that you answer this question before moving out in spiritual warfare. Your compromise will be the open door for the enemy to pummel you and weaken your effectiveness in prayer. Purity is the key to power!

Be sure your obedience is up to date in all areas. God's holy "Brillo pad" is something called confession. All of us want to be God's spokesman in His Holy courts, but He asks that we come with a clean heart. Notice what is taught in Jeremiah 15:19: *"Therefore this is what the LORD says: 'If you repent, I will restore you that you may serve me; if you utter worthy, not worthless, words, you will be my spokesman.'"*

We must do more, however, than merely confess sin. We must be those who root out strongholds in our hearts wherever we find them! The Lord is pleased when we take time to let the Holy Spirit "spotlight" shine on our hearts and reveal those things within us that offend His holiness. Prayer, fasting, asking others to correct us when we err— these are all powerful means to keep our hearts clean and fresh, making us battle ready the strategies of Satan.

We must also discern by God's voice how to detect the enemy's attack and, through prayer, destroy it. Like the servant of Elisha, we must have our eyes opened to the battlefield that is all around us (II Kings 6:15-17). The spiritual Christian should quickly understand any movement in his or her spirit so we can achieve immediately in prayer what God desires. Prayer is work. It accomplishes more than any other spiritual work. It is warfare and battle field power that breaks the back of demonic principalities (Eph. 6:18). Prayer can cast down high level strategies against us.

This warfare praying must be done in certain ways.

1. By revelation, as we are led by the Spirit

God's Spirit must lead us, not the lures of the enemy. The devil is a master at distraction, luring us into battlegrounds that HE chooses. With Divine insight, we can know the issues where victory awaits us as we avoid the temptation to chase after every lure that comes along. We fix our eyes on Jesus, not the devil (Heb. 12:2).

2. In faith

Intercession is not for the faint of heart. We must be filled with faith as we pray, believing that with God, all things are possible. We cannot pretend that faith is in our hearts when we come before dark forces. We must be those who stand in all the armor of God in faith.

3. Directly, boldly, and confrontationally

Jesus Christ won our victory at Calvary. His blood is our boldness, not our past experiences. As we confront demon powers, we can be confident that they will yield to the name and power of Jesus. Every knee will bow before that name (Phil. 2:9-10). When you come against dark forces, remember Jesus always leads us in one continual triumph. The victory is yours. He will protect and cover you in His grace! Declare legal restraining orders in the name of Jesus!

4. With wise discernment

Our enemy is clever. Demonic forces masquerade themselves as messengers (angels) of light (II Cor. 11:13-14). They are pretenders and impostors. True discernment is required to pray effectively. They will seek to counterfeit the work of the Holy Spirit. Irrational feelings can often confuse the leading of the Spirit in prayer. It is in God's light that we receive true discernment (Ps. 36:9). None of us are wise enough or mature enough to discern accurately apart from revelation. Any confrontation and engagement with the powers of darkness will require *true* spiritual discernment. He is a spiritual foe—we must have spiritual understanding to detect him. Not every battle is yours to fight. Some are for you, and some are for others. Some are for today, and some are for tomorrow. Seek wisdom and God will give it (James 1:5).

5. Wearing the warrior's wardrobe

Everything you need to face the devil head on you already have in Christ. God is so kind to let you wear His clothes when you go out to battle! Put on the *armor of God*. You are granted access into God's "closet" to go in and spiritually wear His clothes! Put on what God wears when He steps into battle. You look good in God's outfit!

Each piece of the warrior's wardrobe is put on and maintained through prayer. Put on truth, for the devil is a liar. Put on the breastplate to cover your heart with His golden love and flawless righteousness. Put on the helmet to protect your thoughts from being taken captive into darkness. Put on the good news shoes to run swiftly with the gospel and be at peace with everyone. Take the sword and the shield—they are all the provisions of God for you. Daily put on the armor and daily stand complete in your Jesus-suit! Read Ephesians 6:10-18; Romans 10:15, 13:12; II Corinthians 6:7; Isaiah 11:5, 52:7, 59:17; Hebrews 4:12; and I Thessalonians 5:8.

Be Aware of Your Weakness.

Many try to do spiritual warfare prayer without a deep devotional life in God. The Lord is looking for intimate lovers, not just warriors. A life of intimate devotion and seeking after God daily is necessary for our prayers to be effective and potent. To forget about this is to forget that you have an enemy who will take advantage of every weakness. Jehosophat's strategy for warfare was worship out of weakness (II Chron. 20:21). When we are weak, we are strong (II Cor. 12:7-10). True power for warfare is not because we are gifted, experienced, or clever; it is because we have a great King and God who lives within us! Worshipping God in His holiness will protect us in every battle.

Unless believers appreciate their weakness (know how incompetent we are), we will be deceived. Our blind spots become targets. Our strengths will become places where pride leads us astray. Past experiences help only a little. We must have fresh revelation to wage war. We commit a fatal blunder when we think we are beyond the control or manipulation of an evil spirit. When a child of God becomes "spiritual" (Gal. 6:1) he or she is subject to the influence of the supernatural world. This is why Paul first mentions the need to be "strong in the Lord and in His mighty power" before instructing us of our armor (Eph. 3:16, 6:10). If we think it is our strength, we will fail. *His mighty power* wins the battle in prayer.

After Jesus gave His disciples *"power and authority"*(Luke 9:1-3) to cast out demons and heal the sick, He gave them one parting word: *"Take nothing for the journey —no staff, no bag, no bread, no money, no extra tunic."* Why would He tell them to take nothing? Because He had given them all they needed. *His power and authority* must be their strength, not what they would take for the journey.

Grace is enough to take with us on our prayer journey. We do not have to be sinless human beings to have a fruitful prayer life. We need only the realization that it is God plus nothing. When we are content to be the nothing, God will flow through us in prayer (Rom. 8:26). It is not that we take no things with us, but that what we have in grace is more than sufficient to sustain us.

One of the ways we can be protected in our weakness is to have proper spiritual covering. Being submitted to godly leadership is a basic principle of spiritual warfare. This requires humility, for all of us want to do it ourselves. It is human nature to feel like others will get in our way or restrict us if we decide to walk in teamwork or under spiritual authority.

Remember, if you are about to deal with demonic forces that are rebellious to God's purpose, how can you be protected if you are not in a right spirit yourself (under leadership, good attitude toward those over you, walking in teamwork, leaning on the counsel of others, under prayer covering, etc.)? When we understand our weakness, we are prepared to unite with others for maximum effect.

Maintain Firm, Aggressive Resistance.

The Christian life is one unending engagement with the enemy. You have no option of laying down your arms until you stand before the Lord. Nothing can give more ground to the enemy in your life than a passive spirit! You must deal with this issue for lasting breakthrough. Whenever you detect the devil is behind something, do not let him have his way. Always remember your authority and never back down—**no retreat**! Don't forget to **P.U.S.H.** *Pray Until Something Happens*!

Resistance is crucial in spiritual warfare praying. The best defense is a continual offense. Your enemies will be destroyed if you keep resisting and faint not (II Cor. 4:1-2, Gal. 6:9, Jam. 5:7-8). You should never let the enemy attack and not resist in return (I Pet. 5:8-9). Mighty is One who is in you! They have a word for what happens when you do not resist the enemy; it's called *depression*! Is this what you want? If you do not resist, you will end up depressed and with an unexplained heaviness about your spirit. If our inner man is weak, everything else becomes weak.

A frail spirit leads to fear, which weakens us to stand in the day of battle. We must pray with a strong spirit. As the inner man grows strong by the work of the *holy spirit*, we are able to attack the foe with prayer and wrestling. The muscles grow stronger as we battle the adversary. No longer depressed, we are energized to pray, knowing that our prayers are weapons in God's hands (Ps. 18:32-45).

Determine Which Level of Warfare.

It is important to discern the three levels of spiritual warfare and understand which level you are called to confront. These are all interrelated and in the invisible world. The higher level of confrontation will yield the highest results (breakthroughs). We believe the words of our Lord Jesus that He has given us all authority on earth to enforce the laws of the kingdom of God over the kingdom of darkness. Yet there is a need for maturity and wisdom before many sacred "keys" will be given to the Body of Christ.

Unity, love, holiness, and strategic discernment must all flow in greater measure before the greatest breakthroughs of all come to earth.

1. Ground-Level Spiritual Warfare

This is confronting spiritual powers that molest individuals (deliverance). Jesus has given us all authority to break their hold on any human being. By aggressive, bold prayer and fasting, any believer may exercise the delegated authority of Christ to bind the strongman and plunder his goods. The weapons in his hands have been stripped from him by the cross (Col. 2:14).

2. Occult-Level Spiritual Warfare

This exposes and defeats organized forces of darkness (witchcraft, shamanism, Freemasonry, New Age, etc.). Those with the gift of "distinguishing of spirit" are often able to detect this level of warfare. We need them desperately to arise and be a spiritual nose that sniffs out the work of occult level activity. Every believer has authority to walk in true discernment on this level of spiritual warfare.

3. *Strategic-Level Spiritual Warfare*

Wrestling with principalities and powers in a head on confrontation (Elijah on Mt.Carmel, Jesus in the wilderness, Paul and Elymas) can only be done as the church in a region walks in unity. This prophetic/apostolic power is intensified through intercession and visible unity within the Body of Christ in a city or geographical area. Much wisdom must be exercised before this level of warfare is entered into.

One clear example of strategic level spiritual warfare is Jesus sending out the seventy (NIV seventy-two) to preach the gospel, heal the sick, and cast out demons. This was a massive spiritual assault against the strongholds over a region. At least thirty-five teams of two are sent out, creating a network of simultaneous ministry operating over a wide area as Jesus smashes the demonic structures at many places at the same time. This is a great strategy of attack that will be restored to the Church as we enter the battle of the ages in coming days.

> *Now after this the Lord appointed seventy others, and sent them in pairs ahead of Him to every city and place where He Himself was going to come. And He was saying to them, "The harvest is plentiful, but the laborers are few; therefore beseech the Lord of the harvest to send out laborers into His harvest."*
>
> Luke 10:1-2 NAS

We know this is a wise strategy, for it was Jesus who sent them ahead to the very places that He Himself was about to go and release His miracle ministry. The release of the seventy was not just sending preachers, but the release of a highly anointed ministry directed in strategic attack formation against the web of demonic influence over a region. This upgraded strategy would precede the personal appearance of Jesus Himself in these specific cities. It is as though the seventy were the "breakers" (Micah 2:13) who opened the way, and Jesus was the One who came behind to mop up the enemy's camp completely. The One who broke open was of course Jesus working in tandem with His disciples—His prayer partners!

As they were sent, they were given the task of interceding for laborers to be sent into the harvest. Could it be that Jesus was giving them an example of a strategy that could be repeated by a massive and coordinated spiritual assault in a region of apostolic ministry? And could it be that the "laborers" are really those released in battle formation like the seventy? This is an example of a strategically released force of laborers who are sent in pairs over a region to break the network of power over large regions – men and women who are anointed as sent ones to prepare the way of the true ministry of Jesus as He approaches. Our prayer must be to see the Holy Spirit, the Wonderful Lord of the Harvest, orchestrate this strategic release of ministry over the earth, bringing in the harvest that has been prophesied!

Spiritual Mapping

"What an X-ray is to a physician—spiritual mapping is to intercessors!"—Harold Caballeros, a Guatemalan pastor and spiritual warfare general.

Spiritual mapping allows the intercessor to use "smart bombs." Holy Ghost guided prayers will go right to the underbelly of the enemy when we have done our homework with spiritual mapping. **Spiritual mapping** is *the targeting of our prayers to the historical strongholds of a community, region, or nation.* By revelation, we can receive the target coordinates to obliterate the barriers to evangelism in our cities. God wants to give His warriors "inside" information about why darkness lingers where it does.

God understands spiritual mapping. He told Moses to send out spies into the land to discern its strongholds, evaluate the enemy's strength, see firsthand the walled cities, and the potential for breakthrough (Numbers 13). If we are ignorant of Satan's devices, he will take advantage of us and postpone our victory. *What you don't know can defeat you!* Satan's darkness lingers over our cities because we let him get away with it. We are ignorant of how he has erected strongholds over regions. We ignore the reasons why people have given him the right to remain as prince of the air.

Identifying territorial spirits and a basic understanding of the spiritual history (and destiny) of a city or region is crucial to wage strategic level warfare! Anyone who has visited places like India, Japan, Peru, Nepal, New Guinea, and China can verify the elaborate hierarchies of deities and spirits that rule territorially. These invisible beings are firmly rooted in the culture, cities, homes, and hearts of the people dwelling there. They exercise power over beliefs and behavior patterns of the people. This is true of *every* region governed by dark powers today, including your own!

High-ranking spirits are assigned certain territories, and within that territory they have the ability to interfere and postpone the accomplishment of certain things God has willed (Dan. 10).

Through the Biblical window of Daniel 10, we can see these forces over principalities are called "princes" (the "prince" of Persia, the "prince" of Greece, the "prince" of Bombay, India, etc.). Wherever human beings group themselves together we can expect a territorial spirit to be assigned to deceive and blind hearts to the truth (II Cor. 4:4).

One example of this is found in the book of Judges and the story of Samson. One day as he was going down to the Philistines, a young lion came out of the woods and attacked him (Judges 14). Samson was God's deliverer. This lion was empowered by the spirit or principality over Philistia. They worshipped a sun god that was a lion with the face of a man. This was a sphinx coming out to attack God's mighty warrior. As he conquered the lion, God was winning the battle in the heavenlies over the land.

We should remember that discerning the literal name of the principality in your region is important, but not nearly important as uncovering his activity and dismantling strongholds by strategic level intercession. In Acts 16 Paul discerned that the main barrier to the gospel spreading in Philippi was the interference of a "spirit of divination" dwelling in a slave girl. In the Greek, the word "divination" can be translated *"python."* As Paul identified this obstacle, he was able to cast it out and release a city to hear the gospel. The more specific we can target[1] our prayers the more power they will have in pulling down strongholds.

Be sure to research the historical origins of your community, physical, and spiritual factors of the environment, and significant statues, relics, towers, etc. They can give clues to what is taking place in the region. Ask God for revelation, share it with spiritual leaders, and wait for clear strategies to unfold before acting alone.

Penetrating a Territory

The heart of the apostolic ministry today is the building of something that was not previously there. It is the raising up of a platform for the immediate and future expansion of the purposes of God for a territory or region. Perhaps the classic example of this is found in Acts 19 where Paul was led to Ephesus to penetrate that city with the gospel of Christ. Notice the steps of progress given:

❖ **The impartation of the Holy Spirit** (v. 1-6)

Paul understood that the dynamite of the Holy Spirit would be required to break through the strongholds in the region. The first thing he did was to find those open to the revelation of power in the Spirit of God. Paul prayed, and by the laying on of hands they received the fresh baptism flowing from the throne of God as the territorial strongholds began to crumble.

❖ **The small beginning** (v. 7)

"There were about twelve men in all." Paul refused to be turned aside by only having twelve to begin with. God always starts with twelve and makes them into a great company. Apostolic wisdom does not regard the odds from a human standpoint. This act of starting with twelve was crucial to continue the breakthrough.

❖ **The declaration of the kingdom** (v. 8)

For three months Paul declared and hammered away against the religious spirit in that region. His theme?

The *kingdom* of God. This kingdom declaration was an act of treason in the spirit realm. Paul was boldly inviting others to turn their backs on the kingdoms of this world and turn toward the one true and eternal kingdom of God. The issue in this act of penetration was intimidation. The enemy could not silence the apostolic witness that went forth for ninety days. Paul's clear and courageous announcement that the kingdom had come to that region blasted away in the spiritual atmosphere.

◈ **The discipleship of the hungry** (v. 9-10)

Paul turned away from the obstinate and critical ones as he poured himself into the hungry for two years. This intensive training season brought light to an entire province in Asia. This aspect of territorial penetration cannot be forgotten. Training the future "breakers" is the wisest way to extend light and revelation into a region.

◈ **God's release of supernatural power** (v. 11-14)

God did extraordinary miracles through Paul. Penetration is the partnership of God and man. Extraordinary miracles flowed from the hands of a man full of the power of God. These miracles shook the core of the demonic strongholds (the practice of magic) in Ephesus.

◈ **Validation in the Spirit-Realm** (v. 15-17)

The testimony of demons was that the apostolic ministry through Paul had reached a level of recognition in the spirit realm. Demons bowed to Paul because of his spiritual rank. This authority demands obedience from hostile forces in the territory and breaks the resistance to the Word of God. These spiritual collisions of light and darkness can be expected where God is expanding His kingdom.

❖ The cleansing of the Church (v. 18-19)

When the stranglehold upon the minds of believers is broken, their lives will be changed. Light broke through and the believers confessed their evil deeds and came clean. The demonic powers operating freely in the minds of Christians was shattered through this apostolic warfare (II Cor. 10:3-5).

❖ The increase in power and witness of the Word (v. 20)

As light increased through miracles, teaching, discipleship, power encounters and cleansing of hearts, the apostolic foundations were laid, and the Church could prosper.

Power Centers Must Be Dismantled

If demonic powers prevent an individual from being all that God wants them to be, then they also affect cities, people-groups, and nations from fulfilling their spiritual destiny. These strongholds of darkness must be confronted and denied their right of blinding hearts from the truth (II Cor. 4:3-4). Prayer weakens the hold of these territorial spirits over regions. Their grip is most intense at a "power center." This could be a location (e.g., high place, Masonic lodge, occultic site, Hindu temple, etc.) or past evil activity (broken treaties, crimes, broken covenants, etc.). A person empowered by dark forces (strongman) usually oversees these power centers. This person could be a leader of occultic activity, a criminal, government official, or someone with obvious power to deceive and control the spiritual climate in a region.

To prayer-walk is to "pray on site, with insight." It is a form of directed intercession with the prophetic act of walking on the land. The promise to Joshua was *"I will give you every place where you set your foot."* To set our feet down on the land as we pray and cry out to God is a form of spiritual warfare and receiving our inheritance. After spiritual mapping has been done, prayer-walking is crucial. We can take back the land occupied by the enemy by placing our feet upon covenant promises and literal geographical territory. We expect our prayers to be answered on the very locations where we are pray.

The Holy Spirit is our Helper in prayer. He will give us unusual insight about HOW we are to pray and for what specific areas. The communities of the earth need a spiritual counterpart to the Neighborhood Watch Areas where neighbors watch out for one another and notify the authorities if there are suspicious activities. Watchmen are to watch for the Lord and for His people. To walk over the land is to make ourselves available to the Holy Spirit to show us specific warfare issues that we are to pray over. May we have entire cities in days to come that are under spiritual surveillance as the Lord keeps watch over our cities!

It is always wise to have others with you while you prayer-walk, for we were all meant to succeed in warfare together! Confirmation with others is important, and if possible, from spiritual authorities in the region (pastors, leaders, etc). The watchmen on the walls (intercessors) need to communicate with the gatekeepers (leaders), who can respond and act accordingly. This divine cooperation will lead to major breakthroughs in the spiritual bondage over entire regions.

Identificational Repentance

The Church has been given the responsibility and the power to heal the past. This is released through intercession and identificational repentance. Those who do so are called the "repairers of the breach" (Isa.58:12). As we confront our corporate sins and come before God and men as intercessors as we identify with those who have sinned and repent of the evil done, God releases freedom and forgiveness. Often this comes with remarkable and immediate breakthroughs in the spirit realm. As the past is forgiven, destiny is released for individuals, people groups, cities, and nations (II Chron. 7:14).

For the healing of our land, unconfessed historical sins must be exposed and dealt with. These are the reasons why sin has prospered and why darkness envelops nations. Unconfessed sin always gives Satan a legal right to establish a foothold—this is true for a nation or city, just as it is true for an individual. Iniquity passes down generationally, from one age to the next, until it is remitted and forgiven.

Time does not heal national or generational wounds. Christians are those entrusted with the keys to break the cycle of generational bondage. Our willingness to confess and repent even for sins that were before us, breaks curses off our family, our land, our ethnic group. For further research on the power of identificational repentance, we refer you to a few books: *Healing America's Wounds*, by John Dawson (Regal Books, 1994), *The Powerhouse of God*, by Johannes Facius (Sovereign World, 1995) and *Committed to Conquer*, by Bob Beckett.

Warfare Prayer for the Lost

Many of us have unsaved loved ones that we carry in our hearts, longing for them to know Christ and be a part of His eternal family. How can we most effectively pray for them? What about our co-workers, friends, and neighbors who are lost and will die one day without knowing the beauty of our Lord Jesus? As priests of the Most High, we must speak on their behalf and storm heaven with prayer for their conversion.

It is time to take our authority in Christ, turn away from thoughts of self, and pray for the lost. The youth of this nation must turn to Christ. The forgotten peoples around the earth must have a chance to hear the gospel. We must stand in the place of Christ as His prayer partners and plead for the unsaved to come to Christ. God will help us, and He delights to answer our prayers for the salvation of the lost (Luke 19:10, Mark 10:27).

From reading John 3:16, II Peter 3:9, I Timothy 2:4, and other Scriptures, we can be convinced that as we pray for the lost, we are pleasing God and releasing miracle power to draw others to the Cross of Jesus. Think of this: as you pray, you are preparing the soil of the heart for the seed of the Word. Your prayers turn away darkness from others and unlock their hearts to hear the truth. Prayer is a mighty force to turn hearts to God!

The basis of our praying must be the blood of the Cross that purchased souls for God. The right of redemption was won at Calvary. Warfare praying for the lost stands on that ground and intercedes with passion for those who are perishing. Praying in the name of Jesus is asking for and claiming what the blood has paid for – the souls of others! With the prayer of faith we boldly insist that the enemy *give them up* and the Holy Spirit *draw them in*! Our intercession makes this happen as we stand against all the works of Satan that are holding them back (e.g., tradition, unbelief, false teaching, new age philosophies, hatred, etc).

The unsaved are blinded (II Cor. 4:3-4), and our prayers aid in opening their eyes to the light of Christ. It is time to lift up Jesus high over the hearts of our loved ones and those who are lost. Cities can be won through prayer. Families can be spared through prayer. The wayward sons and daughters will return through believing, warfare prayer.

Studying the Warfare Portions of Scripture

I Chronicles 12 catalogs more than 340,000 courageous, valiant fighting men. These are David's mighty men who with their loyal troops protected and defended God's anointed King. Equipped with weapons and unswervingly devoted to righteousness, these men had responded to the call to stand with David and see the kingdom brought into reality. Much revelation can be found for warfare intercession in this chapter.

Another portion of Scripture that is designed to enlighten the Church for warfare victories is found in II Chronicles 20. Intercessory praise defeats the enemy as the armies of God march out to do battle. Worshipping warriors will be those whom God anoints to defeat the enemy. Many times it is the singers, musicians, dancers, and poets who first understand what God is about to do. They are anointed with creative wisdom to discern demonic activities and heavenly strategies to defeat them. Who of us has not been touched deeply by the words of the worshippers who sing and compose songs that move our soul? Yes, praise is a powerful form of spiritual warfare.

Other warfare Scriptures that are waiting to be unlocked and used in battle include the books of Joshua and Judges, Numbers 32, I Samuel 17, Psalm 18, Psalm 149, Ephesians 6, and Revalation 12-19.

Declaration of God's Victory and Breakthroughs

Spiritual warfare is a ministry of declaration. This is really a war of words: God's words vs. Satan's lies. Intercessors are to praise and worship, bind and loose, but the time will come when God will use the *declaration* or shout of triumph to bring down a stronghold (e.g., the walls of Jericho). Spiritual warfare is more than just prayer to God; it is a declaration to the enemy that God has triumphed! These bold, anointed declarations become spiritual weapons to topple strongholds.

The building of the Temple in Ezra's day was accomplished through the decrees uttered by the people of God. Something broke through in the heavens as God's people gathered in unity and decreed the completion of the house of the Lord. These warfare decrees are spoken by both the saints and by the agents of the enemy. Faith in the stated purposes of God will release divine energy to complete the work God has called you to do. The day of building is a day of strong decrees (Micah 7:11). This is the heart and power of governmental prayer.

The enemy's declarations are lies, fiery darts, and arrows of ambush. It is the powerful proclamation of the *word* of God (both "logos" and "rhema") that dismantles his power hold. Remember, the Ark of Covenant (the Divine Presence) that Israel took with them into battle had the written tablets of the Word of God hidden within.

In Genesis 3:15 there was a prophecy given by God concerning the intercessory ministry of the Church.

We are told that the seed of the woman will crush the head of the serpent. This speaks of God giving the Church the authority to deal with the attacks of the enemy. Since we belong to Christ (Gal. 3:26-29), we are part of this promise of the overcoming seed! We have kingdom authority to tear down strongholds, push back darkness, and establish righteousness on the earth. It's time to serve an eviction notice on the dark powers over our cities!

It is time to declare the supreme triumph of Jesus over all the works of the enemy. We, the blood-bought Bride, have the authority to declare and implement this victory through intercessory prayer. Our cries release the *"sound of chariots, horses and a great army"* in the camp of the enemy (II Kings 7:6). The mingling of prayer and worship releases the beauty realm, but the mingling of prayer and declaration releases the thunders of the throne!

The dynamics of intercession include the capacity to deal with the powers of darkness. It is the prayers of the righteous that stir up the activity of God on earth. Intercessory prayers and bold declarations of God's victory have helped birth every revival! One of the best illustrations of this type of prayer warfare is given in Joshua 10. In order to pursue and conquer the enemies of Israel, Joshua commanded the sun to stand still in the sky. This enabled the armies of Israel to rout the enemy in broad daylight. This chapter yields great insights for intercessors.

Perhaps the greatest warfare declaration of the New Testament is found in Roman 16:20. *"The God of peace will soon crush Satan under your feet. The grace of our Lord Jesus be with you."* The Church is given this prophetic declaration to use over the activities of Satan. They will all be thwarted and crushed under the faith-walk of believers who stand on this declaration! Get ready to walk over every work of the enemy in your life, your family, church, and your region!

---

[1] For those interested in spiritual mapping, we encourage you to read two books. George Otis, Jr., has written two books entitled *The Twilight Labyrinth* (Chosen Books, 1997) & *"Praying with Power"* by C. Peter Wagner (Regal, 1997). They each point out the three basic questions to answer in spiritual mapping: What is wrong with the community? How did it get this way? What can be done for it?

Weapons of Our Warfare

*With weapons of righteousness
in the right hand and in the left.*
II Corinthians 6:7

As you come to God in believing prayer on behalf of others, there will be times when you will face the powers of darkness. Your God, your Captain, has not left you defenseless. Mighty weapons are at your disposal. A proper understanding of the power of these weapons, and how to use them with skill against your foe is crucial for victory. You must become one who tears down strongholds wherever you find them. In this way, you loose others to fulfill their destiny. Your battle on earth stirs Divine intervention in heaven. You are more than a match for the devil—**Jesus** lives in you!

Your arsenal is complete. God has given you *every* weapon you need for warfare and intercessory authority. Your part is to *use* these weapons with courage. God's Word guarantees your victory! The heavenly believer knows how to use the Word of God to break down the enemy's lie.

Beware of using tactics of the flesh to battle powers of darkness! The demons will not bow before you; it is the **Mighty Jesus** in you that strikes terror in their hearts.

Some of the weapons of the world that must forsake include the following:

◈ Human reasoning, our own thinking

◈ Praying our desires—this is soulish, not spiritual

◈ Forcing our will or arguments upon another

◈ Manipulation, using the fear of rejection on others

◈ Deception, any distortion of the truth for our own ends

◈ Control, binding others emotionally to us.

These are all the ways of the flesh, the way the world does battle. Our weapons are spiritual and mighty to the pulling down of strongholds! Examine the weapons God has given to us in His Word. *Here is your arsenal:*

Our Foundation: Faith and Obedience

The *foundation* of spiritual warfare is *faith and obedience*. These twin virtues are the pillars of victory when you face the enemy on any level. Faith and obedience are intertwined and work together—they are incomplete without the other. You must have *faith* that the weapons God has given you will work, demolishing all hiding places of the enemy.

Faith is essential in crushing doubt, fear, and darkness. Without faith you cannot please God or conquer the enemy. *Obedience* to the Spirit of God and to the Word of God is required for every warrior of Christ. God will entrust to you responsibilities in the Spirit that you must fulfill. You must be obedient to what God gives you—or you will not entrusted with more. Your very life must be a statement of *faith* and *obedience* to the kingdom of darkness or you will retreat in the face of their fury!

Faith and obedience activate all of the weapons. When you take the Name of Jesus, the Blood of Jesus, and the Word of God and mix them with faith, you have the greatest arsenal in the universe. The very power of God flows through faith. Faith is your victory, faith is your shield, faith is your boldness (Mark 11:22-24, I John 5:4, Eph. 6:16, Heb. 10:22).

God tells us that we have been given "weapons of righteousness in the right hand and in the left" (II Cor. 6:7). Faith and obedience are these righteous weapons! How do they work? When you face accusation from the enemy or any opposition to your spiritual advance, faith must rise in your spirit. Without bold faith you will drown in the accusation of the enemy. Faith rests in truth, accusation in lies. Believe the truth of God and resist the devil in faith (I Pet. 5:9). Never listen to accusation but always respond with faith to the whispering lies of darkness:

Accusation of the Enemy	*Respond with Truth*
"Who do you think you are"	"God calls me His Beloved!"
"You have no right to do this"	"God clothes me in His Power!"
"You haven't prayed enough"	"God is my confidence "
"You can't stand before me"	"The Mighty God lives in me!"

Faith and obedience are indispensable for your walk of victory. DO NOT listen to lies; feed your heart with the truth of God. Determine right now that your life belongs to Christ and that you will not be moved or shaken (Ps. 46:1-3).

Our Authority: The Name of Jesus

Everything has to bow before the name of Jesus! The name of Jesus has power on earth, in heaven, and in hell! Since you are a walking temple of the Living God, you can use the name of Jesus as though He Himself with all His authority is standing beside you (I Cor. 6:17)! Your King Jesus has given you the authority and power over demons, and you now have the right to ask the Father for victory in His name (Luke 10:19).

"And I will do whatever you ask in my name, so that the Son may bring glory to the Father. You may ask me for anything in my name, and I will do it" (John 14:13-14). Use the name (Power and Virtue represented by the name) of Jesus in warfare as you intercede God recognizes that name and will answer you. The demons recognize that name and tremble (Psalm 18:45). Make the enemy flee in terror! Speak the names of Jesus over the strongholds of darkness. Use this weapon beloved! The power of the Holy Spirit is released when you take up the names of Jesus.

This can be likened to a police officer wearing a badge, taking authority to stop vehicles many times larger than the police officer. Intercessors who wear the badge of the name of Jesus can stop the schemes of Satan by using His Glorious Name! To use the names of Jesus in warfare is to use the keys of authority *in His names* to unlock the power of God. Using His name authorizes you to use His authority in every place you encounter darkness.

We are using the revelation of *who God is* when we use His name on the battlefield. Inner fears and crippling doubts flee when we understand who God is. At His name, angels bow, demons flee, and hardened hearts melt. The climax of human history will be the unveiling of the glory of the name of Jesus. His name is great and greatly to be praised! Read Philippians 2:5-10.

However, there is a warning attached to using the name of Jesus. To have authority in the Spirit to use this name requires an intimate and personal relationship with Him. Your fellowship with Jesus in secret gives you power over darkness. To use the name of Jesus as a good luck charm will get you into trouble! It is not enough to use the name of Jesus. We must have the nature of Jesus in our hearts.

If your life is in disobedience or compromise, you are using God's name in vain! Power comes from relationship. Peter and James used the name of Jesus to heal the lame man at the Gate Beautiful (Acts 3:1-8). They were known as men who had been with Jesus and absorbed His life. The glory of His name is seen in the fruit of His life coming forth from you.

The seven sons of Sceva tried to use the name of Jesus without a relationship with Him. They were beaten and bruised by demons (Acts 19:11-17). How many times have you been beaten and bruised by the enemy? Could it be that you were praying in the name of Jesus with hidden compromise in your life? Authority and power flow through relationship. Under His shadow, we cast down strongholds. Apart from HIM we can do nothing.

Our Covering: The Blood of Jesus

We have representation in heaven at the highest level. Our Great High Priest has brought His sacred blood before the Father's throne and purchased our boldness. We are not uncovered or vulnerable as we pray; we are covered in the blood of Christ.

The subject of the blood of Jesus in Scripture is astonishing. From Genesis to Revelation God has used the blood of innocence to atone, cover, and remove guilt. Where guilt has been removed, power flows! The blood of Jesus, like the blood of the Passover Lamb, drives away the death angel (Ex. 12:22-23). Dark powers are stripped of their weapons where the Blood of Jesus is applied.

The Blood of Jesus is *His life in sacrifice before the Father*. The life is in the blood. The shed blood of His Cross releases the indestructible and endless life of Jesus. It cannot be overcome—the blood of God conquers dark princes. One drop of His blood had enough power to redeem all of humanity from the chains of sin. Imagine how the demons see the blood? Here are some of the things the blood of Jesus does for *you*:

◆ The Blood of Jesus *saves us* (Eph. 1:7).

◆ The Blood *justifies* us before God (Acts 13:38-39).

◆ The Blood *sanctifies* (set us apart) (Heb. 10:10,14).

◆ The Blood *reconciles* us to God (Col. 1:20).

◆ The Blood has *overcoming power* (Lk. 10:19, Rev. 12:11).

◆ The Blood *cleanes* from all sin (I John 1:7).

◆ The Blood *releases* New Covenant power (Heb. 7:22, 8:13)

◆ The Blood *delivers* from darkness (Col. 1:13-14, 2:15).

To use the blood of Jesus in warfare and intercession is to stand identified with the complete acceptance of the Lamb. The perfections, the glory, the life, the righteousness of the Lamb of God are conveyed in the blood. This weapon will never fail. Blessed is the intercessor who knows how to use the power of the blood in spiritual warfare. To apply the blood of Jesus is to remind the enemy of his boundaries, of his failures and weaknesses.

The blood of Jesus does to the enemy what lies of accusation does to you. Give it back to him! Remind the enemy of the power of the blood! Push him back with the crimson wave of power—the blood of the precious Son of God! In the fiercest fight against the dark forces, the blood of Jesus will work for you. This is the overcoming power at your disposal.

You are safe in the "bubble" of the blood. You are protected from the onslaughts of the enemy. The power of the blood removes all fear. In the first Passover, the blood of the lamb gave supernatural protection. They obeyed the word of the Lord and sprinkled the doorpost with blood. Many mental, emotional, physical, and spiritual plagues are loosed against the believer in this day. It will be the power of the blood that will keep you safe in the "bubble." The Israelites had to stay under the blood to be protected. So we must we!

Our Testimony: The Word of God

The Word of God coming from our mouths has an dramatic impact on the spirit realm around us. Jesus will one day strike the nations and rule them with a rod of iron. He is seen in Revelation 19:113-15 as One who is called the Word of God and "out of his mouth comes a sharp sword with which to strike down the nations." The Word of God coming from His lips becomes a sharp sword with which to wage war and govern nations. There is power for spiritual dominion in the words we pray!

Everything you do in intercession and spiritual warfare must be based on the Word of God. His Word abiding in you gives you wisdom for warfare, strength for the battle, and faith to combat your foe (John 15:7-8). You must learn to use the Word of God as a sword against dark powers (Eph. 6:17). The more you know and confess the Word, the more effective will be your victory. Here are some ways you can use the sword of the Spirit:

◈ Quote the Word to the enemy; remind him of his defeat.

◈ Quote the Word to the Lord to affirm His promises.

◈ Ask God for a word of direction for the person/situation.

◈ Allow the Spirit to use the sword in your own heart first.

It is impossible to overstate the importance of the Word of God in our prayer life. Words are the containers of our faith. They are powerful to demolish strongholds. As we are in combat with demonic darkness, and as the Word of God dwells richly in us, we have ample ammunition to discharge against any attack.

Ignorance of the Word of God leaves us defenseless. Jesus, the Incarnate Word, used the written word when He was tempted by the devil. If Jesus needed the Word, then so do I. Some Scriptures are direct weapons for warfare. These include the promises of God, the prophetic prayers, the apostolic teachings, and the Book of Revelation. However, there are two sections of the Bible that give us extraordinary power and weapons for warfare:

The Psalms

Various psalms are given to us to increase our effectiveness in spiritual warfare. The enemies that pursued David are a picture of the spiritual enemies that hinder us. You may find it helpful to substitute our spiritual enemies (sin, sickness, self, Satan) for the natural enemies of David and Israel. These psalms give strategy, comfort, and wisdom when we are faced with spiritual opposition (e.g., Psalm 18 and 149). Read them carefully and underline the principles you see for warfare prayer.

Every believer should have at least 6-10 psalms memorized and written upon his or her heart. The truths they implant within you will be joy and strength for your prayer life. Here are some psalms that have uniquely touched my life. They have never failed to encourage me heart and release divine activity in my soul:

- Psalms to pray for the outpouring of the Holy Spirit: 44, 65, 67, 80, 83, 102, 110

- Psalms to pray for overcoming personal defeat: 6, 13, 25, 42, 43, 51, 69

- Psalms to pray as an aid for your devotional life in God: 25-27, 45, 61-63, 84, 103, 138

- Psalms to pray-read, looking for spiritual warfare direction: 8, 16, 18, 27, 42, 61-63, 90-92, 103, 107, 121-150.

The History of Israel

Exodus through Chronicles is the historical account of how God dealt with Israel and the unfolding of His purpose for His people. Joshua and Judges give incredible insight into battlefield strategies. *Every* believer needs to have an understanding of these books and where they fit in the panoramic purpose of heaven. Joshua is the Old Testament form of the name *Jesus!* Read through the books of Joshua and Judges as though they were manuals for spiritual warfare. Take note of the different strategies God released to His leaders for war. Take note of their defeats as well as their victories. You will learn much from the historical section of the Old Testament. Everything written is for our example and instruction (I Cor. 10:6,11).

Joshua 10 is perhaps the most powerful example of spiritual warfare and intercessory prayer in the Word. This chapter records the epic battle between the Israelites and five kings of the Amorites. After an all night march (watch of the Lord), Joshua took his enemies by surprise. God helped out with heavenly artillery! Hailstones fell from the sky as Joshua executed judgment on his enemies! More were killed by the hailstones than by the swords of the Israelites. By the declaration of Joshua, the sun stood still so that warfare could be completed!

His Word Worked for Me!

The "word of their testimony" (Rev. 12:11) is the specific truths of God that have delivered the saints. Our testimony is that the *word of God worked* for us! There is no victory apart from the Lord and His Word. The word of testimony is the word we use to testify of God's power! Here is a sample "word of testimony" that is sure to push back the devil:

I TESTIFY TO SATAN PERSONALLY:
That the Word of God has set me free!

I stand before You covered and sprinkled
in the precious blood of Christ.
Through the blood of Christ
I am redeemed from the hand of the devil.
Through the blood all my sins have been forgiven
And this blood continually cleanses me from sin.
Through the blood of Jesus I am set apart *for God.*
I carry His authority
My body is a temple of the Holy Spirit.
Satan, you have no place in me.
You have no power over me!
The blood of Jesus has been shed for me!

Our Banner: *Praise and Worship*

Praise and worship are effective weapons of spiritual warfare. They open the heavens for revelation, for power, and for God's Spirit to flow. Praise opens prison doors and sets our souls free again (Acts 16:23-26). Jesus taught His disciples to start and end prayer with praise. We worship God not *after* the victory, but to get the victory!

Praise lays the groundwork for the forces of heaven to move on our behalf. You battle *from* a place of victory. Praise is the ground of victory beneath your feet. Stand in the garments of praise! How does praise help us in warfare?

◈ It draws you into His presence where you can receive wisdom and strength (Ps. 100:4).

◈ It opens doors in the heavens releasing the activity of heaven on your behalf (Isa. 60:18).

◈ It paralyzes forces of darkness and defeats the devil (II Kings 11:13-14; Ps. 8:2, 149:5-9).

❖ It brings revival (II Chron. 31:2, 34:12; Ps. 107:32).

❖ Praise is God's address, where He may be found (Ps. 22:3).

❖ Praise is a garment ;it clothes us in the Spirit (Isa. 61:1-3).

❖ It is the way into Christ's victory (Ps. 106:47, II Cor. 2:14).

❖ Praise is a sacrifice we offer to God (Jer. 33:11, Heb. 13:15).

When you clap your hands or march or lift your hands in praise, you are waging battle in the heavens. Worship and intercession are weapons in the Spirit to wreck havoc on your enemy. Prophetic worship is a mighty instrument of war for the trained believers. If you are facing an enemy in the spirit and you do not know what to do, praise your way into the realm of spiritual victory. Praise and worship win our battles.

Praise is a weapon that will release captives and bring in the harvest. Use your worshipful weapons of warfare and watch them set free the hearts of others. God sent King Jehoshaphat into battle armed only with this song: "The Lord is good and His mercy endures forever!" As we sing our praises, the music becomes a weapon for GOD to wield. Heavenly foes are conquered when God's people lift their hearts to Him in song (Isa. 30:32). Even the harvest of souls we are crying out for will come when all the people *praise the Lord.*

"May the peoples praise you, O God; may all the people praise you. THEN the land will yield its harvest, and God, our God, will bless us" (Ps. 67:5-6).

Worship and intercession must flow together to dismantle strongholds in the heavenlies. This is the ministry of the harp and bowl described in the heavenly scene of Revelation 5:8-9: *"And the twenty-four elders fell down before the Lamb. Each one had* **harp** *and they were holding* **golden bowls** *of incense, which are* **the prayers of the saints.** *And they sang a new song...."* This is the mingling of worship and intercession that results in loosing judgments upon the kingdom of darkness.

So often, simply by our anointed worship and fervent intercession, the victory is ours. The battle is won in the heavens as our hearts agree with God through worship (the harp) and intercession (the prayers of the saints). New songs will flow as we enter into the "marriage made in heaven" of our prayers and our worship. Perhaps every Christian and every church is given a bowl that must be filled with intercession (incense). Prayer fills a golden bowl. May our praises and our prayers arise as sweet incense before the Lord!

Our Internet: The Prayer of Agreement

As an intercessor, you must agree with the Holy Spirit as you pray. Likewise, we are to pray in agreement or harmony with others. If we are in strife with others in the Body of Christ, our prayers will be ineffective and without punch. Learn to pray in agreement with other intercessors before tackling difficult spiritual issues (Matt. 18:19-20, Acts 2:1).

Jesus sent his disciples out two by two. They were sent with power and authority to cast out demons and plunder the kingdom of darkness. Having agreement with others in prayer (unity) is a vital weapon for spiritual warfare. When we are alone, we become an easy target. If we have an independent spirit (rebellion), we are powerless to face our foe. Praying in agreement with others keeps us from deception and protects us from an assault. We need to go "on-line" with others in the Spirit and have unity in our declarations.

You may want to find a prayer partner to form an alliance with them in the spirit. One can chase a thousand, but two can chase ten thousand! Such an alliance can greatly multiply your strength in warfare. But *choose a prayer partner wisely*, under the direction of the Holy Spirit. Make sure the relationship is pure (same sex), holy, and above reproach. Are there hidden motives or agendas? Would the Lord be pleased? Learning to pray in agreement is praying in the will of God. Do not agree with the lies of the enemy; agree with God's Word in prayer.

Our Secret Weapon: Praying in the Spirit (Jude 20)

There are two ways we can understand the value of praying in the Spirit:

1. Prayer in the Spirit is to follow the leading of the Spirit in prayer. He imparts direction and communicates how to pray and what to pray for. This is prayer that follows God's prompting.

2. Prayer in the Spirit is your human spirit praying directly to God in your devotional life of intercession and worship (I Cor. 14:2). Some call this "praying in tongues" or a "prayer language." This is not to be confused with the *gift* of tongues (I Cor. 14), which must have an interpretation in the church. This prayer language is a devotional tool that enhances your spiritual perception and releases power in your inner man. Under this anointing, the intercessor may see a vision or hear a word of direction, caution, discernment, or strategy.

Many testify that praying in the spirit is a perfect prayer. Since we do not always know what to pray for as we should, praying in the spirit is a God-anointed prayer, even if we do not understand it. These are some of the "mysteries" of our spirit (I Cor. 14:2). Praying in the spirit becomes a way for the Holy Spirit to pray His prayers through you; this is His prayer language that is shared with you (Rom. 8:26-28). Even though you do not understand what you are praying, God does, and it becomes a spiritual weapon to break through the forces of darkness (I Cor. 14:10 and Eph. 6:18).

If you pray in tongues, it is important that you *do not criticize* those who don't. The issue is not *how* you pray, but your heart attitudes in prayer! Many faithful prayer warriors do not have a prayer language, as it is called, but they have powerful, effective lives of prayer. If you are one that does not speak in tongues *do not criticize* those who do (I Cor. 14:5,18,39).

Our Cutting Edge: Fasting (Isaiah 58)

"Christian fasting, at its root, is the hunger of a homesickness for God."—John Piper

"More than any other discipline, fasting reveals the things that control us. This is a wonderful benefit to the true disciple who longs to be transformed into the image of Jesus Christ. We cover up what is inside of us with food and other things."—Richard Foster

"Fasting, if we conceive of it truly, must not be confined to the question of food and drink; fasting should really be made to include abstinence from anything which is legitimate in and of itself for the sake of some special spiritual purpose."—Dr. Martin Lloyd-Jones

"Some have exalted religious fasting beyond all Scripture and reason; however, others have utterly disregarded the discipline of fasting."—John Wesley

"Man does not live on bread alone, but on every word that comes from the mouth of God."—Jesus

Coupled with prayer, fasting is a potent weapon in the believer's arsenal. More than just abstaining from food, it is an act of self-denial for higher purposes. Fasting increases your spiritual power; it frees you from the flesh and increases the level of authority in the spirit realm. FASTING IS THE WAY TO POWER (Luke 4:1,2,14).

Jesus set an example of fasting for forty days without food. The three major miracle workers of the Bible (Moses, Elijah, Jesus) all fasted forty days. It is a spiritual discipline that increases the release of the Spirit in your life and ministry. This sensitivity to the Holy Spirit causes you to be powerful in intercessory / warfare prayer (Acts 10:30-31).

Some of the benefits of fasting include the following:

◈ Fasting is a means to receive guidance and direction from the Holy Spirit (Dan. 9; Acts 13:1-3, 14:21-23).

◈ Fasting brings the blessings of obedience (Matt. 6:6,16).

◈ Fasting brings great victories. King Jehoshaphat called a national fast against invading armies, and the enemies killed each other! See II Chronicles 20:1-30.

◈ Fasting will give you greater authority over demon spirits (Matt. 17:20).

◈ Fasting is a glorious way to get close to your Lord. It increases your receptivity to the Lord in dreams and visions. Spiritual intimacy is intensified during a fast.

Jesus began His earthly ministry with a forty-day fast. The Spirit of God led Him into a wilderness where He would find power for His ministry. As a Man anointed by the Spirit, His extended fast prepared Him for a miracle ministry. But of course, He is the Son of God. What about you and me? Can we really enter into the grace of fasting? Is it something Jesus would want us to do?

When fasting is properly understood within the Scriptural context, it becomes attainable for everybody in the Body of Christ. The enemy would either keep us afraid of fasting or make us so extreme about fasting we abuse the grace God would give us. A lifestyle of putting God first will one day lead us to the door of adventure. This furious love, which has conquered our hearts, must be given back to the Lord Jesus. There is a place of radical love for Jesus Christ that will impart grace to suffer for Him, grace to go without legitimate pleasures, grace to give Him everything.

It is always best to fast with a specific goal. Focus your prayers during a fast and watch God work. What is really accomplished by fasting? Probably more than you will ever know until you get to heaven! Make fasting a lifestyle habit and you will become mighty in prayer!

Our Intelligence: Spiritual Discernment (II Cor. 2:11)

In active spiritual warfare, the most critical information is not what you know, but what you do not know. What you do not know can kill you, especially if your enemy knows you don't know it. We cannot afford to be ignorant of the devil's schemes. We must have discernment. Both to know what God is doing, and to know what the enemy is scheming. It can be fatal to step into a "hot zone" of spiritual warfare unawares.

Prayer warriors must know where to engage the enemy. Ignorance is costly. Christians can become war casualties when they least expect it—where they think they are out of danger. This is why many Christians are wounded in the safe place of their home or church. To them the battlefield was somewhere else.

Our real enemy is Satan. You cannot afford to be ignorant of how he wages war. You must have discernment! He is the inventor of spiritual guerrilla warfare. Lacking true authority to defeat us, he resorts to seduction, deceit, lies, subversion, and trickery (II Tim. 2:25-26, John 8:44, Eph. 2:1-3).

The success of the devil's schemes depends on one thing: ignorance. He uses stealth to come in undetected if we are not discerning. Some of the saints misread James 4:7 to make it say, "Ignore the devil and he will flee from you." We are not told to ignore the enemy but to *resist* him—*resist* the devil and he will flee. Our focus is always on Jesus, our King, but we must be astute and enlightened by the Spirit of God to know the devious schemes of Satan. The enemy will use our ignorance (lack of discernment) to neutralize our effectiveness in prayer.

We urge you to educate yourself in spiritual warfare. None of us have all the pieces or all the understanding needed to win every battle. Jesus is our Captain, the One who has broken through for us to release every perfect weapon. Our Captain has taught others about warfare; they are mighty men and women of the Spirit. They have written books in the last ten years that offer incredible insight. Be a student of the Word of God, but do not be afraid to upgrade your understanding by reading books like *That None Should Perish* by Ed Silvoso of the Argentina revival. *Taking Our Cities for God*, by John Dawson, offers much insight for "city-reachers."

Uncovering the Devil's Strategies to Keep You From a Life of Prayer!

One more time: the devil *hates it when you pray*! His name means "adversary" and "opposer." Satan will do anything to keep you from prayer, the place of true power. He is cunning, devious, and relentless in his attack against your prayer life. For a disciple of Jesus, prayer is not a pastime—it is a passion. We must be alert to the various strategies he uses to keep us from prayer. Here is how he attempts to distract you:

1. Keeping you busy with religious activities

2. Incredible physical fatigue every time you pray

3. Distracting thoughts and interruptions

4. Emotional issues
   a. Struggling with hurt feelings
   b. Sense of failure, inadequacy, and condemnation
   c. Anxious fears
   d. Cold, detached feelings that numb the spirit
   e. Indifference, feeling that it does not matter

5. Misinterpreting God's ways

6. Praying for the wrong things
   a. Selfish prayers.
   b. Thinking we know God's will for others
   c. Limited spiritual perception—immaturity

7. Making us angry toward spiritual leaders

8. Physical attacks

    a. Dizziness
    b. Inability to focus
    c. Headaches
    d. Pain in the body
    e. Deafness
    f. Inability to speak
    g. Unable to breathe

9. Disturbing your environment
    a. Family pressures
    b. Financial stress
    c. Uncertainty or anxiety at work
    d. Unnecessary conversations during prayer times

Go through this list again and ask the Holy Spirit to show you the specific strategy the enemy has used against you the past seven days. Put on the armor of God and refuse to let it happen again!

Breakthrough Prayer

*Righteous Father, though the world does not know you,
I now you, and they know that you have sent me. I have
made you known to them, And will continue to make you
known In order that the love you have for me may be in
them And that I myself may be in them.*
John 17:25-26

The greatest prayer of all time is found in John 17. It was the prayer of our magnificent Intercessor, Jesus Christ spoken in the Garden of Gethsemane on the night He was betrayed. Knowing He was going to be delivered up that night to be condemned and crucified, He spent His night on earth interceding for us. This is the most prophetic prayer in the Scriptures. It is a prayer that will yet be answered by God the Father for His end-time Church. The Father Himself is committed to answering the prayer of His dear Son. Every request in this prayer will be fulfilled before Jesus returns.

Jesus prayed the breakthrough prayer for you! No one has interceded like Jesus Christ for His beloved Bride, the Church. Flaming zeal in His heart prompted Him to pray for you before He was crucified. You were in His mind the night He was betrayed. Desire for you to know the Father filled His soul. Ponder this prayer found in

John 17. Pray this prayer and allow the Holy Spirit to give you understanding. But there are numerous strategies and models of intercession found in the Scriptures.

Prophetic Intercession

"If they are prophets and have the word of the Lord, let them plead with the Lord Almighty" (Jeremiah 27:18).

A radical new breed of humble, broken-hearted intercessors are rising up in the church. They are powerfully prophetic and have learned how to touch the heart of God. Many are hidden in secret—praying night and day for revival, for righteousness, for the destiny of nations, churches and leaders. We may be seeing the joining of the priest and the prophet. It is time for the "Anna company" to arise and pray the prophetic promises back to God!

Anna was a hidden but significant prophetic intercessor who was on hand when Jesus was offered in dedication as an infant. Extravagantly devoted for as much as sixty years to intercession and fasting in the House of the Lord. This was one praying widow! As one who dwelt in the secret place of intimacy with God, she was made aware of the times of transition and the appearing of the Christ. She will have a place in history as one who waited and prayed and believed until the Promise came.

We see her in at 84 years old, still seeking God fervently (Luke 2:36-38). Something was burning in her heart to keep her praying with passion all those years. There is no record of any prophecy she spoke, but she was a woman of the secret place.

The expression of her prophetic ministry was in her enduring intercession for the redemption of Jerusalem. She prayed through the prophetic promises of God. She was given revelation, and she prayed until she saw it fulfilled. These "praying prophets" are anointed to bring change in the spiritual climate around them. Though not limited to women, this company of kingdom-pullers seems to follow in the steps of Anna. They give birth, they travail, and they labor in prayer. This is their call; this is their joy.

Are you one who will pray until the prophetic destiny of others is fulfilled? Our Father is seeking for priests who will plead the cause, thus paving the way for prophetic promises to come to pass. Every unfulfilled promise must be brought before the Lord by prophetic intercessors. This is the call of the Anna Company. This revelatory praying is the ability to receive divine information from God and plead with Him Christ is the heavenlies (Eph. 2:6).

These prayer partners with Jesus see with heavenly eyes and pray until His will is done. It is entering into the intercessory ministry of Jesus Christ. Seated with Him, they see from His viewpoint. Their intercession flows from revelation. Their prayers become swords and weapons. It may begin by something as simple as a burden to pray. Yet the burden does not go away, for God is giving you a prayer assignment.

The heart of the intercessor becomes the womb where God's purpose labors to come forth. The intercessor becomes a focused warrior, "conspiring[1]" with God to release His glory in the earth! The prophetic intercessors seen in the Old Testament include Esther, Daniel, Deborah, Joseph, and Jeremiah. They had divine revelation as they laid hold of prophetic promises until they were fulfilled. You must ask the Lord, "Is this my call? Is that what you are drawing me into?"

God is searching today for men and women who will take their place on the wall with a sword in one hand and a trowel in the other. Will you arise and become one of His radical revolutionaries? Will you be the answer to His plea?

Apostolic Intercession

The Church of Jesus Christ is returning to the fire and passion of the first century. This apostolic move of God is taking firm hold in the earth and bringing renewal and restoration to the foundations of churches. Fresh revelation for relevant preaching is pouring forth from the Word of God, and a fiery, passionate form of prayer is being birthed in our day that will unlock the heavens over nations and cities. Apostolic Intercession is now here!

The Scriptures fuel the fires of prayer. As we take the written, infallible Word of God and make it our vocabulary in prayer, we soar to the heights God intends. When the Word and the Spirit are united, we are given wings to fly! Suddenly our weary hearts are lifted on eagles' wings, taking us into the jet stream of divine purpose. What is apostolic intercession? It is the prayer model of the apostles of Jesus.

Governmental or apostolic prayer is the prayer of faith and declaration. It is a proclamation to the principalities and powers of the enemy's camp of what God is about to do as we ask in faith. It is breakthrough prayer—authoritative and powerful—bringing a shift in the heavens. This type of prayer has momentum and spiritual force. It blasts through the defenses of the enemy and results in accomplishing the will of God. See Isaiah 14:24-26.

The Breakthrough Factor

It is time to take prayer to the breakthrough level—the place of Divine response. We must not be content to leave our prayer life on the religious level of merely something that we must do to be spiritual. David prayed and the heavens shook and the voice of God was clearly heard. This is the breakthrough factor that must be reached in our day.

> *In my distress I called to the LORD; I called out to my God. From his temple he heard my voice; My cry came to his ears. "The earth trembled and quaked, The foundations of the heavens shook; They trembled because he was angry. Smoke rose from his nostrils; Consuming fire came from His mouth, Burning coals blazed out of it. He parted the heavens and came down; Dark clouds were under his feet. He mounted the cherubim and flew; He soared on the wings of the wind He made darkness His canopy around him-The dark rain clouds of the sky. Out of the brightness of his presence bolts of lightning blazed forth. The LORD thundered from heaven; The voice of the Most High resounded.*
> 2 Samuel 22:7-14

This kind of prayer stirs God to move and hidden things are uncovered. God is seen upon the wings of the wind as He races to break through and create the miracle prayed for. Every time your prayer is answered, God mounts the cherubim and thunders His decrees from heaven on your behalf. The results we see in the natural are only the outer wrapping of the power He displays in the spirit realm in response to our urgent prayer.

As we search the New Testament for examples of apostolic or breakthrough prayer, there are some patterns that surface. The book of Acts is meant to be a manual for prayer ministry in the Church. It begins and ends with prayer. Here are some of the obvious models of intercession found in the book of Acts:

◈ The apostles established places and times for prayer.

◈ The Early Church was faithful to pray for its leaders.

◈ Prayer was a ministry they were devoted to.

◈ Corporate prayer was practiced in many different forms.

◈ They prayed in homes (cell groups).

◈ They prayed as they walked.

◈ They were quick to pray at any time, any place.

◈ Worship and prayer were practiced routinely.

◈ Fasting and prayer was their custom.

◈ They prayed authoritatively against evil.

Stretching Out in Prayer

One of the major calamities that came against the Early Church was the persecution of Herod. The evil king wanted to bind Peter in prison and thus paralyze the church. Herod recognized the anointing and authority of this apostle and knew that Peter must be dealt with. This one prisoner was guarded by sixteen soldiers, but the church entered into unceasing prayer over the situation. The Greek word used in Acts 12:5 for "unceasing" for "fervent" prayer is literally "stretching out in prayer." It is the word from which we get the English word "tension." It means to "stretch out in prayer" with a "tension" in our activity that stretches the boundaries and vibrates the spiritual realm until something pops; something gives; something breaks through!

It is as though the mighty prayer of the saints keeps a tension on the enemy until he yields and God's purposes stand. This "stretching out in prayer" is a strong determination that something must yield. The saints who prayed in Acts 12 knew that Peter's deliverance in the natural was unlikely and probably would never happen. Herod intended to either keep Peter in prison all his life or to kill him. But the believers in Mary's house knew that they had a secret weapon, a stretching prayer that could change physical reality and bring a heavenly break-through. They broke through so Peter could break out! They expected God to answer in a dramatic and powerful way.

They were totally unaware that God had already broken through—they just kept the tension, stretching their souls out in prayer! They had no word of knowledge or angelic activity to tell them to stop praying. No evidence was there that God had performed the miracle until Peter actually turned up outside their door! This heavenly prayer model actually created a new reality on earth, breaking through the natural boundaries (prison doors), and released miracle power. Their insistent stretching out in prayer accomplished the work, and it even took them by surprise! Can you imagine what would happen if this kind of prayer was restored to your church. No more boring prayer times and half-hearted whimpers; a holy hum begins to rise as the saints "stretch out in prayer," causing our "Peter" to turn up at our gate!

Another instance where breakthrough prayer broke the chains was in Acts 16. We find the apostles in prison for preaching the gospel and planting churches. In their prison cell at midnight, Paul and Silas released governmental prayer and sang the high praises that released the two-edged sword

> *May the praise of God be in their mouths And a double-edged sword in their hands, To inflict vengeance on the nations and punishment on the peoples, To bind their kings with fetters, Their nobles with shackles of iron, To carry out the sentence written against them. This is the glory of all his saints.*
>
> Psalm 149:6-9

Their breakthrough prayer of praise and faith blasted into demonic territory and broke the stronghold over that jail! The very foundation of the demonic realm was shaken as the whole city was broken open. Salvation is released to the jailor (possibly the Macedonian man Paul saw in his vision). Even the magistrates who had beaten Paul and Silas came pleading with them to leave their city peacefully. The power over Philippi was destroyed, and the city leaders came humbling themselves to the governmental power of God in His apostles.

When the church in a region begins to cry out to God using the apostolic example, revival and glory will dwell in the church. To help us follow this model, we have listed below examples from the New Testament. Please look up (and pray) these Scriptures for your fellowship of believers.

- **Ephesians 1:17-19** — Pray for the Holy Spirit of Wisdom and Revelation to be expressed in our lives as we welcome His truth, conviction, and transforming power. Pray that every truth we learn will lead us into a deeper knowledge of Christ. Pray that hope will fill our hearts, convincing us of our destiny in Christ. And pray for power that will overcome even death.

When this prayer for the revelatory spirit to fall on the church is answered, the Church will come into the fullness of His glory.

- **Ephesians 3:16-19** — This prayer is for the supernatural strength of God to come into our being as the Holy Spirit is released within us. Faith is the virtue that will bring more of this into our life, so pray that God will increase your faith. As you grow in love, Jesus comes forth within you. Ask Him for His love to be revealed to you.

- **Ephesians 6:18-20** — This is a prayer for the release of boldness and anointing for public ministry. God wants His servants to carry His Word with courage to the ends of the earth. It will require fresh measures of boldness to carry it out. Signs and wonders will be done on earth as the Church moves into Holy Spirit boldness in the prayer room.

- **Phil. 1:9, I Thess. 3:12, and II Thess. 3:5** — Pray for an increase of love in the body of Christ. Only the release of the Spirit can accomplish this. He will reveal our brokenness and weaknesses that we may lean upon Him. Pray that all gifts will flow in love as we seek the blessing of others. God will give us the wisdom of the Spirit to walk in these things.

- **Colossians 1:9-11** — Pray that God would make known His will to His people as the Holy Spirit is released upon us. The people of God need spiritual understanding to grown and fulfill the purpose of God. Pray for power to be patient in hardships.

- **Colossians 4:2-4, Acts 14:27** — Paul requests prayer that God would open a door of evangelism through the release of His anointing upon the Word. There is a door of opportunity that our prayers must knock on if we want to enter into anointed evangelism. Jesus opens these doors as we intercede in faith (Rev. 3:8). Corporate prayer must turn to the lost. Doors of opportunity swing open as the Church prays. The opening of doors releases miracles, signs, and wonders by the Holy Spirit.

- **Colossians 4:12** — We must pray for spiritual maturity to come to the church across the city. This type of intercession raises the level of spirituality in a region. There is a measure of grace and maturity that will only come as we pray. This brings God's will to the earth.

- **I Thess. 3:10, II Cor. 13:9, Heb. 13:20-21, and I Cor. 1:8** — These are prayers for the Church to be established, complete and mature. It is only by the release of the Spirit that these prayers will be answered. Spiritual fruit, gifts, and wisdom come as the Holy Spirit overwhelms our heart with transforming grace.

- **Rom. 15:5-6, and John 17:20-22** — Unity among the saints! This must be prayed down as we ask the Holy Spirit to make us one in all things. We need intercessors to pray these prayers until the leadership of the Church models the unity of the Trinity.

- **I Cor. 1:4-8** — Paul's apostolic prayer is for the church across a city to excel in spiritual gifts as they await the coming of Christ. Revelation knowledge and citywide strategies will be birthed. The Church will grow in maturity and be blameless in the day of Christ.

- **II Cor. 13:9** — This is a prayer for the church of the city to grow in maturity, wisdom, and all the dimensions of the grace of God. How right it is to pray this for your region!

- **I Thess. 1:2-3, II Thess. 1:3** — Prayers of thanksgiving for the grace given to others will bring MORE grace to them and enlarge our hearts in love. It is crucial that the Church prays with thankful hearts as we ask for even more!

- **I Thess. 3:9-13** — The Church is to pray for the release of apostolic ministry to the whole Church in that region, causing the believers to abound in love and holiness. Mature ones must come and complete what is lacking and immature in the Church of a region. God's plan is to make us holy and blameless when Christ returns.

- **I Thess. 5:23-25** — We must pray for passion for Jesus and purity of heart. The Holy Spirit will empower us as we pray this way. The faithful God will be stirred to activity to protect and cleanse our lives and our churches.

- **II Thess. 1:11-12** — Our corporate times of prayer must include asking God to equip us in His grace for the glory of God. Only He can make us worthy of the high calling He has placed upon us. As we partner with Jesus in prayer, we fulfill the will of God and the work of faith with power.

- **II Thess. 3:3, and James 4:7** — This is the closest we find to warfare praying in the New Testament. These apostolic prayers are for the power to overcome, resist, and defeat dark strategies in human hearts. Satan, the evil one, is defeated in our lives as we pray and stand on God's promises. Our praying must be within the sphere of authority given to us as believers.

- **II Thess. 2:17** — Pray that God would strengthen us to fulfill God's will. Comfort will come to the Church as we pray to the God of everlasting hope. This prayer will release the power of God for change, the wisdom of God for direction, and the conviction of God to remain faithful through life's pressures.

- **II Thess.3:1-5** — It will be prayer that delivers believers from persecution. Intercession digs a channel for the power and the Word of God to flow in. We must build a house of prayer in every city, asking the Father to protect from the evil one, to establish the saints, and for the love of God to be poured out.

- **II Cor. 13:7-9, I Thess. 3:10-13, and Phil. 1:9** — Praying these Scriptures will release to the Church purity, love, and holiness. We must arise with these words in our mouth and pull down the virtue of heaven into the Bride of Christ. The Bride makes herself ready when she walks in these strengths. The release of Spirit will bring this to earth.

- **I Tim. 1:17, 6:15-16** — This is a worship prayer. It speaks a blessing upon God and pleases His heart. The Father longs for worshippers who will pray. This type of prayer answers the longing of His heart and the desires of our hearts to connect with eternity.

- **I Tim. 2:1-4** — We are given the responsibility to pray for government authorities and civil leaders. This prayer releases peace and tranquility to the Church in a city. It pleases the Father that you would pray for their salvation and the salvation of all men.

- **II Tim. 2:7, 24-26; Luke 24:45; and Acts 16:14** — We must ask God to open the hearts of others and grant them repentance. Jesus holds the keys; prayer opens the hearts. This prayer for revelation and understanding must be a theme of our prayer.

- **Acts 4:24-31, and Eph. 6:19** — These are prayers for boldness. There is a measure of boldness we will never have if we do not ask for it! Boldness is a specific manifestation of the Holy Spirit that is imparted through prayer. The united prayer of apostles will release the hand of God for healing, signs and wonders.

- **Matt. 9:37-38, and Luke 10:2** — Laborers! The harvest is great but few are those who will become His "reaping angels." We must rise up and pray for anointed laborers to be sent to the nations of the earth and bring in the harvest. Those who are full of the Holy Spirit—full of His gifts, fruit, and wisdom—will fully answer this prayer.

- **Rom. 10:1** — A prayer for Israel that they would receive the knowledge of salvation in Christ. Paul's prayer was earnest and from his heart.

- **Rom. 15:5-7** — This is a prayer for unity of the Church within a city. The faith to unite churches in a region will be expressed by fervent, apostolic intercession. Only God's Spirit can answer this prayer.

- **Rom. 15:30-33** — There is a need for united, fervent prayer to secure the deliverance and freedom from persecution for those who preach the gospel. Our prayers can make it safe and fruitful for the outreach of the gospel to go forth.

- **II Thess. 3:1-2** — Prayer multiplies the power and anointing of the spoken word. We must have an increase of power upon the preaching of the gospel and the teaching of the saints. As the Holy Spirit falls, anointing increases our effectiveness.

- **II Thess. 1:11-12** — We must pray for the maturing of the body of Christ by receiving a greater grace than we now have. Prayer releases heaven's substance on earth. We will only be found worthy and fulfill our calling as we enter into partnership prayer with Jesus.

- **Eph. 3:18-19, II Thess. 3:5** — This is the great prayer of Paul for an increase of the revelation of love in the churches. This deep, transforming revelation comes by the power of the Holy Spirit.

- **Phil. 4-6** — Prayer activates evangelism. Sharing our faith is a bold step that comes as the Church unites in corporate prayer. Faith must arise in the prayer meeting if we would walk in faith to preach the gospel. Full understanding will come to us as we pray in faith.

- **Heb. 13:20-21** — This is a prayer acknowledging the greatness of God, His covenant of love with us, and the power of the resurrection of Jesus. We pray out of this revelation. As we intercede, a greater level of maturity will come to the Church and bring glory to our Great Shepherd.

- **James 1:5-6** — Praying in faith releases divine wisdom. The Church will not walk in wisdom if we will not ask for it. As we pray, true understanding and discernment flows. There is no reluctance in the Father's heart to give His kids whatever they ask for.

- **III John 2** — Spiritual and physical health comes as the beloved church prays. Our personalities (soul) will prosper and come alive before God, reflecting the image of Christ. The God of Abraham will bless everything in our life as we intercede in His love.

- **Jude 20, and Eph .6:18** — This form of prayer will release strong faith within us. It includes praying with boldness, in the Spirit, and with the knowledge that we are His beloved one. We must pray for the saints to have the faith needed to go to the next level in God.

Other New Testament Examples

New Testament prayers are focused and specific. Generic, non-specific prayers really accomplish little. As we search the New Testament, we discover some valuable lessons for our prayer life. Paul and all the apostles were men of prayer. Their lives were spent in the word of God and praying for the needs of the churches (Acts 6:4). We must have leaders today who value these same things:feeding our souls in the Word so that we may give to others, and a satisfying prayer life that is filled with intercession for others.

Pray the Beatitudes. As you pray for others use the kingdom truths of Matthew 5:3-12. Take the truths Jesus taught and pray them for your spouse, your pastor, your loved ones:

*Blessed are the poor in spirit, for theirs is the kingdom
of heaven. Blessed are those who mourn, for they will be comforted. Blessed are the meek, for they will inherit the earth.
Blessed are those who hunger and thirst for righteousness,
for they will be filled. Blessed are the merciful,
for they will be shown mercy. Blessed are the pure in heart,
for they will see God. Blessed are the peacemakers,
for they will be called sons of God.
Blessed are those who are persecuted because of righteousness,
for theirs is the kingdom of heaven....
Blessed are you when people insult you, persecute you
and falsely say all kinds of evil against you because of me.
Rejoice and be glad, because great
is your reward in heaven...."*

You could pray like this: "Father, help John to be
who is pure in heart. Let him be one who sees You in all
things. Make him a peacemaker where there is strife until
he is seen be others as a son of God. Work meekness into
his heart today." Each of the "blessings" of the beatitudes
should be prayed over for others, even for your own life!
The Lord loves to hear us pray His Word. We can even
sing our prayers as the angels sing before the throne (See
Revelation 4-5 and Ephesians 5:19-20.)

Holy Pleadings

This is an intense form of intercession where the
intercessor comes before the Righteous Judge and to Jesus
the Mediator of a New Covenant (Heb. 12:22-24). This is
our plea before the mercy seat for God to move on our
behalf. The "courtroom of heaven" is waiting for intercessors to come with holy pleadings, where Jesus our
Advocate takes us by the arm and presents us to Judge of
all the earth!

*"Put Me in remembrance and **let us argue** our case together. State your cause and let us argue our case together. State your cause that you may be proved right"* (Isa. 43:26).

*"Come now, **let us REASON** together"* (Isa. 1:18, Job 23:3-7).

Presenting your case and laying out your arguments pleases God. He invites you to do this in prayer. Do not just pray meaningless words. Take the Word of God and put God in remembrance of what is written. This will cause you to be moved with compassion. It engages your heart in your intercession. Your determination will be strengthened as you come into His presence with your just cause. Those who prevail with God are those who bring forth their reasons and strong arguments. Faith wrestles with God until He blesses us. These "holy wrestlings" are the expressions of a burning heart in love with His Name.

This holy debate becomes a passionate presentation of the many reasons why God should answer our plea. We never plead as an adversary, but as His friend. Petition the court of heaven for an injunction against Satan to end his harassment. The Advocate with the Father will give you the words. Praying the Scriptures is basic for every intercessor. When you pray the prayers of the Bible, you are praying a perfect prayer. We are not pleading for our will, but for God's will. His will is revealed in what He has written.

One of the anointed intercessors of today, James Goll, has given in his timely book *Kneeling on the Promises* seven Scriptural foundations for these holy pleadings:

Seven Ways to Make an Appeal before God

1. *"For the Honor and the Glory of Your Great Name!"* God saved Israel at the Red Sea for His own name's sake

(Psalm 106:8). Samuel and David used this appeal as they interceded before God (II Sam. 7:26; Ps. 23:3, 31:3, 109:21, 143:11). We lift our voice to ask God to move by His Holy Spirit and vindicate the honor and glory of His own great name.

2. *We plead God's relationship to us.* God is our Creator, our Father, and our Redeemer. We remind Him that we are the work of His hands (Ps. 119:73). God is called our Helper (Ps. 33:20, 40:17, 46:1). As our Father, He will have compassion on us (Isa. 64:8, Rom. 8:15). He will protect and cover and bless His redeemed!

3. *We plead God's attributes.* God, You are Righteous. God, You are loving. We can plead His great faithfulness as Ethan did in Psalm 89. Mercy—plead His mercy (Deut. 9:18; Ps. 4:1, 27:7, 30:10, 86:6; Daniel 2:28). You will find the attributes of God to be as it were a battering ram, which *will* open the gates of heaven on your behalf.

4. *Plead the sorrows and needs of the people.* David wept for the suffering of his enemies. How much more should we for our friends. As we identify with the sufferings of others, we take on the nature of Christ, the True Intercessor. The book of Lamentations is Jeremiah taking on the sufferings of his people and pleading for God's intervention. In desperate circumstances we may cling to the heart of His mercy for His people (Ps. 137:1-4).

5. *Plead according to the past answers to your prayers.* David reminded himself and God of how He had helped in the past (Ps. 27:9, 71:17-18). What God has done in the past, He is able to do today. Be faithful to bring past mercies into view as you plead with God (Ps. 78, 105, 136). Recite the times He has prevailed over your enemies. Plead for power to be manifested.

6. *Plead the Promises of the Word of God.* His Covenant promises of Scripture are for YOU. Urge Him to fulfill them in your need. David held God to His Word, reverently, with holy insistence—press the Lord for their fulfillment (I Chron. 17:23-26). Solomon must have learned this from his father (II Chron. 6:14-17).

7. *Plead the Blood of the Cross.* The most powerful tool for the intercessor is the blood of Jesus' cross. There is no prevailing argument we can bring to the throne. We have no merit. We do not prevail by our techniques. It is the power of the blood that will unlock the heavens for you! Let there be a generation of intercessors who take the blood of the Cross as their cry, "God, give us a blood-washed America!" One drop of the blood of Jesus is more powerful than anything the enemy has in his arsenal. See Exodus 12:5-23, Romans 5:9, & Hebrews 10:19-23.

Praying Down Miracles

God is waiting for intercessors to cry out for the miracles He has reserved for the last days. We must become those who pray down the power of God. Those in Third World nations today are coming to Christ as a direct result of some kind of supernatural encounter. Church planters overseas confirm that miracles are the tools God is using to give birth to churches in the nations of the earth. When prayer becomes a habit, miracles will flow! Here are some prayer strategies for praying down miracles in your city:

1. Pray for God to reveal Himself in a vision to those you pray for. Believe it will happen.

2. Pray for God to anoint His servants with power for healing.

3. Unite with others for prayer with the purpose of asking God for miracles in your city.

4. Pray for God to heal cancer victims and those with HIV.

5. Pray for a visitation of God for those on their deathbeds.

6. Pray for entire families and neighborhoods to come to Christ.

7. Pray for dramatic conversions of those in the cults.

8. Pray for Jesus to visit your church services to save the lost.

9. Pray for signs in the heavens to confirm His Word.

10. Pray that Jesus reveals Himself to witches.

11. Pray that dreams will warn unbelievers to come to Christ.

12. Pray for newspaper and television staff to become Christians.

13. Pray that Jesus appear to those seeking false gods.

14. Pray that those visited by God would seek out believers to disciple them and join churches.

15. Pray for Jesus to visit government officials and military.

16. Pray for God to visit future church leaders with power.

17. Pray that those who persecute believers would be visited by God and converted.

18. Pray for revival in the prisons and orphanages.

19. Pray that churches in your area identify ruling spirits and receive strategy to topple them.

20. Pray for the dead to be raised by God's power in your city.

Other Prayer Teachings of Jesus

Jesus is our Magnificent Intercessor. There is none who can compare to Him. His life of prayer is the perfect model for us. His teachings on prayer need to be received and walked out in church life today. Here are just a few of the examples and teachings of our Lord Jesus Christ on the subject of prayer:

◈ Jesus prayed long hours alone, often during the night (Matt. 14:23; Luke 5:16, 6:12).

◈ Jesus prayed for strength in the time of testing and temptation (Matt. 26:40-41).

❖ He teaches us to pray for justice to prevail. God is faithful (Lk. 18:1-8).

❖ Jesus prayed for strength for His disciples in their time of testing (Luke 22:31-32).

❖ Jesus constantly demonstrated His willingness to heal in answer to prayer (Matt. 8:1-4).

❖ Jesus was quick to answer even the peculiar faith-prayers of others (Matt. 8:5-13).

❖ Under pressure, Jesus is always there to sustain us in prayer (Matt. 8:23-27).

❖ Jesus allowed people to interrupt His teaching with their request (Matt. 9:18-19).

❖ On His way to raise the dead, He healed in answer to prayer (Matt. 9:20-22).

❖ In answer to prayer, Jesus empowers us to do the impossible (Matt. 14:28-30).

❖ Bold, persistent, not-giving-up prayer will be answered (Matt. 15:21-28).

❖ The prayer blessing of Jesus will use our limited resources for a miracle (Mark 6:41).

❖ Wisdom for leadership selection and development comes through prayer (Luke 6:12-13).

❖ Prayer delivers from temptation as we partner with Jesus (Luke 22:39-46).

◈ Jesus prayed to keep you protected by the power of the Father's name (John 17:11).

◈ Jesus prayed that we both be *one* with each other *and* one with Him (John 17:11, 21).

◈ Jesus prayed for you to be set apart in holiness (sanctified) (John 17:17).

◈ Jesus prayed for you to experience the fullness of the glory of God (John 17:21-26).

---

[1] The word "conspire" means "to breathe together."

The House of Prayer

*These I will bring to my holy mountain And give them joy
in my house of prayer. Their burnt offerings and sacrifices
Will be accepted on my altar; For my house will be called
A house of prayer for all nations.*
Isaiah 56:7

The Lord Jesus Christ is looking for a place to
live—a place where He can dwell, not just visit. His house
will be called a house of prayer. Jesus is going to be found
on earth wherever there is night and day prayer ascending to the Father. These prayer experiences will not only
be a delight to God, but it will, be enjoyable for His people. Enjoyable prayer is coming to a church near you! God
will be the source and sustainer of this joy. Here are some
features of enjoyable prayer:

◈ Prayer, rooted in the assurance that God enjoys you!

◈ It is *throne-centered prayer* flowing out of the beauty
realm of God. Love-sick worshippers see God as our
very great reward! God is the portion for the Levites;
He is their inheritance.

◈ It is prayer that finds our true reward in Him, not just in revival or miracles or healing, as we see Him in His indescribable beauty (Gen. 15:1; Isa. 4:2, 33:17).

◈ It is prayer that is established in holiness. We will come to His **"holy mountain"** with a happy holiness that abandons every dark way and crooked thought.

◈ Extravagant giving and a love without price tags will make prayer enjoyable for God's people. Our **burnt offerings and sacrifices** (missions, giving to the poor, fasting, etc.) will be pleasing to God.

◈ A new identity for the church is coming—a house of prayer, a prayer center for all nations. As we pray around the clock, the Great Commission will be fulfilled in our generation!

Did you know that the devil keeps a 24-hour watch? He does not sleep but accuses the brethren day and night. Day and night accusation must be answered by night and day intercession! Just as the devil stands before God night and day accusing the saints, the Church must stand before God night and day and agree with God. This night and day agreement with the Father will be known as the house of prayer. This is the house that Jesus built, and the gates of hell will not prevail against it!

The House of Prayer

It is time for us to become a House for the Lord, a habitat for divinity. In city after city the Holy Spirit is inspiring His people to build houses for the Lord to move into. As the city church invites God to dwell in their region, the life and glory of Jesus will come. The Father's

House is truly to become a house of hrayer (Matt. 21:13). As we partner with the Lord Himself, God's highest purposes for our cities and nations will be realized. Heaven waits for earth to build from living stones a habitat for divinity!

The church in a city must become a divine stronghold, a place where God's manifest presence is established. The Lord has a burden to rivet His presence to the earth in 24-hour-a-day prayer centers. These habitats for divinity will release a continuum of God's radiant presence over regions and territories of the earth.

Divine strongholds will one day be known as places where the Lord's power is manifested in healing, regional unity, extraordinary signs and wonders, and worldwide harvest.

The Lord has promised to rebuild "David's fallen tent," which is the 24-hour prayer model that began on Mt. Zion with an unveiled Ark (God) in David's backyard! This prayer model will be recaptured by the end-time Church with worshippers and intercession filling the heavens above the major cities of the world! See Acts 15:15-18.

There are twenty-four elders mentioned in Revelation 4-5, and there are 24 hours in a day and 24 time zones around the earth. Global worship and intercession will release global harvest as we cover the earth with praise and fill the golden bowls of heaven with fragrant incense.

Imagine what will happen when we begin a ministry on earth that is modeled after the ministry on the sea of glass! Worship in the high place will move outward releasing victory and triumph to the earth. Does your heart leap with joy over joining such an orchestra of worship?

Watch AND Pray

The words "watchmen," "watchman," "watch, watching," "watchful," "watcher," and "watches," are found 165 times in the Scriptures. Jesus tells us to "watch AND pray," implying that watching and praying would be distinct although similar activities. Every believer has the ministry of one who is to watch and pray. God is the One who has divinely set this before us. It is God's will to raise up faithful watchmen and set them in place as holy sentinels for His purposes.

You must become one who watches for the Lord. We are His divinely posted "look-outs" who will see the enemy before he attacks. We will be those with the first glimpses of the Lord as He approaches His people with revival. The cities of our land and the nations of the earth are waiting for the God-appointed watchmen to take their places. Our charge from Isaiah 62 is simply this:

1. Give yourself no rest. Don't stop until the answer comes.

2. Give Him no rest. Wrestle in prayer until God lets you "pin Him."

Our intercession is to be persistent, determined, intense, energetic and prevailing. As God's reminders, we come before Him night and day on behalf of God's people. The understanding of salvation is released as we pray and keep watch for the nations.

Fiery, holy intercession must be the pattern of our lives. We are to be those who make up the hedge and build up the wall in a time of battle.

From Isaiah 59:16 we learn that God expects somebody to stand in the gap and come before Him pleading the people's case. He is surprised when this does not happen. If there is no intercessor, evil and judgment may fall. Intercession turns back evil and makes a hedge of protection around the people (Ps. 94:16). It does not say that

God looked for an evangelist or a pastor; He looked for an intercessor!

Our God is so eager to hear your prayers and answer them that He says in Isaiah 65:24, *"Before they call I will answer; while they are still speaking I will hear."* In fact, He wants us to constantly come before Him and "give Him no rest." He so loves being asked by His longing Church that He sets people on the wall and appoints them to "never be silent day or night!"

God the Father is THE WATCHMAN who keeps watch over the cities, nations, and peoples of the earth (Ps. 121). He watches over His Word to perform it (Jer. 1:12). He watches over the destinies of His beloved ones (Gen. 16:13, 28:15-21). He watches over the heavens and the earth to assure that all is according to His plan (Ps. 33:14). He watches us when we hurt and need a miracle (Ex. 3:16, Deut. 2:7). There is no watchman like God Himself! Every wise watchman on earth has an example in the Fathering God. We can be watchmen because He is watching. We are created in His image—the Chief Watchman!

The Magi that came to Jesus at His birth were watchmen. They were watching the heavens for a sign. The angels announced Jesus' birth to shepherds who were watching over their flocks by night. This was a prophetic sign that the Shepherd-King would come and keep watch over His flock, and today He is calling His pastor-shepherds to also keep the night watch as they guard the precious flock of Jesus.

Simeon and Anna were watching for the coming of the Lord as His parents brought Jesus to the Temple to be dedicated to God. They were intercessors who fasted and prayed for eyes to see eternal purpose as it was brought before their eyes. Great was their privilege to see and hold the baby Jesus and gaze into the eyes of the God-Man.

At twelve years of age, Jesus was a Watchman who had to be in His Father's House (Luke 2:49). Jesus spent His life watching the Father and doing only what He saw the Father doing. He spent nights in prayer, days in prayer, having fellowship and communion with the One who meant most to Him, the Father.

Jesus was the Man the Father looked for—*the man* who would *"build up the wall"* and stand before Him *"in the gap"* (Eze. 22:30). Jesus was the One who interceded and intervened on behalf of you and me. As we follow in His steps, we too will become watchmen on the wall.

I believe the Lord Jesus is still wanting to take His disciples along with Him to spend a night in prayer, just as He did with Peter, James, and John in the Garden of Gethsemane: *"Stay here and keep watch with me"* (Matt. 26:38).

Jesus could sleep in a boat on a troubled sea, but in the Garden it was time to watch and pray. Jesus' eyes were so much on the Father that He could not be distracted by a spirit of slumber. Jesus lay awake all night to pray. May He help us to stay alert and watch with Him until He comes as a Bridegroom!

Watchmen on the Hilltop

In Exodus 17:8-15, there is a story of Joshua fighting in the valley and Moses praying on the hilltop. As Joshua was going head-to-head with the Amalekites, Moses was holding a rod over the battle with his arms held high. As watchmen-priests, Aaron and Hur came to hold up Moses' hands when he grew weary. As long as the hands were lifted up holding the rod, Joshua would win down in the valley.

The battle was both physical and spiritual. Joshua had to fight the physical battle with his troops in tactical deployment. Moses had to fight the spiritual battle praying strategic prayers as he watched from the high place.

The rod of God was the assurance to the troops fighting below that God's purpose would stand. God was watching over His armies through Moses, Aaron, and Hur. Everyone's role in this battle was significant and crucial for ultimate victory.

Spiritual leaders today must be covered by strategic prayer. Intercession protects them and keeps their swords sharpened. It is dangerous in this day to be a leader without a team of faithful armor-bearers (intercessors) surrounding them.

There are some in the body of Christ who are called to take a strategic position of a personal intercessor for leaders in the church. These are the "Aaron and Hur holding company" who lifts up the arms of the captains in battle. They are called alongside of leaders to bless, encourage, uplift, and intercede.

How many battles have we lost because there was no one to watch and pray for God's warriors in the battle? How many spiritual leaders have fallen on the battlefield because of no one to lift their arms? May this be the day of commissioning! May our Mighty Captain give these intercessory assignments to the "Aaron and Hur holding company" of today!

Building a Prayer Wall

Every prayer, every groan, every cry is a part of *hedge-making* and *wall-building* so that others may stand against the enemy. We are to pray and work for the rebuilding of the moral and spiritual walls of protection around people and nations (Isa. 57:14). Intercessors are the Ezras and Nehemiahs of today that take a bold stand for righteousness.

With God's authority, our intercession takes a firm stance against the enemy and commands him to vacate strongholds and hiding places he has deceitfully entered. We have the authority to bind and loose by our prayers. Intercessors can crush the enemy's schemes before they are unleashed.

Look out! Here come God's end-time intercessors. With a militant, reckless abandonment, they will stand for the Lord and for the *lost*! Are you ready to get radical for prayer?

Intercessors must remind the Lord of His promises around the clock—never holding our peace until He establishes His righteousness on earth (Isa. 62:6-7). We must *know* God's agenda and like His secretary, remind Him of His appointments. Our prayers become a wall to keep out demonic hindrances. If ever our nation needed intercessors it is now. The future belongs to the intercessors. It is time to pray!

Isaiah 21:6-12 provides an interesting understanding of the "watchman ministry" of an intercessor. The Lord instructs Isaiah to post lookouts or watchmen who will be fully alert and at their post night and day: *"Go, post a lookout and have him report what he sees... let him be alert, fully alert!"*

Intercessors have strategic assignments given to them by God to scour the spiritual horizons like air traffic controllers. In prayer, God will expose the strategies of the darkness and show the enemy's cards that he intends to play (Jer. 51:12).

Listen to what was asked of Isaiah, the prophetic seer: **"Watchman, what is left of the night?"** People are looking to those who spend time with God to know what is ahead. People are longing to know who has the heart of

God for what is coming.? "Is the enemy near?" "Is there danger out there coming our way?" "When will this be over?" The Church is crying out for the night to end and the dawning of the true day to come forth.

The honest reply of the watchman is given in verse 12: **"Morning is coming, but also the night."** The morning of new opportunity is coming to the earth. Yet so also is a night of calamity. The counsel of the watchman is that this is no time for trifling or playing games with God. If you are going to pray, you'd better pray. **"If you would ask, then ask."** If you ever said that one day I am going to be a man/woman of prayer, then this is that day! It's time to get right with God and **"come back yet again."**

The Watch of the Lord

The watch of the Lord is one of the ancient tools God is restoring to the Church. It is a powerful strategy of intercession that will unleash fresh power to the earth. This is an overlooked model of prayer. Matthew 26:41 says, *"Keep watching and praying that you may not enter into temptation; the spirit is willing, but the flesh is weak."* The "watch" is a military term used to define segments of time during which a sentry guards a city from harm— alerting the citizens of approaching enemies. These guards would remain on their watch until it was completed and another gatekeeper comes and takes his place (Isa. 21:6-9).

The night would be divided into four watches of three hours each. Mark's gospel speaks of the "fourth watch of the night" (Mark 6:48). Jesus still comes to His people in the watches of the night. But are we those who look for Him? Are there sentries on duty in our city, watching the churches and needs of others? Let us put out the welcome mat for the Holy Spirit to invade our cities. Let us become those who are "possessed for prayer." See Lamentations 2:18-19.

The Greek word for "watch" means, "to be vigilant, alert." This is our responsibility in prayer—to be vigilant and alert. Eleven times in the gospels we are told to watch and be alert. Paul also tells us to "continue in prayer and watch with thanksgiving" (Col. 4:2). It is time to restore the watch of the Lord. Intercessory watchmen must arise and take their place on the walls of our cities. As we stay awake all night long, the enemy cannot find an entrance. If there is one on duty, we can catch him red-handed!

Notice the watches in Scripture:

- Exodus 14:24 — the morning watch, which includes warfare

- Psalm 101:8 — watching over the city all night

- Psalm 130:5-6 — waiting and watching for a visitation

- Acts 3:1 — specific hours of prayer in the Early Church

- Psalm 55:17 — morning, afternoon, and evening prayer

- Isaiah 62:6-7 — Giving Him no rest

- Luke 18:1-7 — Crying out day and night

- Habbakkuk 2:1-3 – Watching and recording the vision

- Proverbs 8:34-35 — Watching, listening, and waiting on the Lord

- Ephesians 6:18 — Staying alert and praying at all times

- I Peter 4:7 — Watching with a sober Spirit

- I Peter 5:8-9 — Being alert, resisting the devil, standing firm

- Revelation 3:2 — Waking up and bringing life out of death

- Matthew 26:41 — We are tempted but prayer is a key to escape!

- Revelation 16:15 — Watching in prayer clothes us with power!

- Matthew 24:42-44 — Watching in prayer for the Bridegroom!

- Revelation 20:1-3 – The prayer chain that binds up the serpent

Unceasing Prayer

May this holy baton be passed from one generation to another as we wait for the Lord to crush the great serpent under His feet! May the watchmen take their places on the walls crying out to Him night and day. May each of us become a part of building a wall of prayer around our cities!

Enthroned Intercessors

*And God raised us up with Christ And seated
us with him In the heavenly realms in Christ Jesus.*
Ephesians 2:6

It would be impossible for God to give you more
than what you already have in Jesus Christ. Beloved, you
are blessed with everything heaven can give (Eph. 1:3)—
not when you die,but *right now!* You are as ready for
heaven as you will ever be! Fully justified, fully forgiven,
you are God's beloved child. He likes you! He loves to
hear your voice and calls it lovely (Song of Songs 2:14).
You look like Jesus when you come before the Father. He
receives you and loves *you* just like He receives and loves
His Son, for you are "in Christ" (Eph. 1:6). How does it
feel to be accepted just as you are?

Your inheritance as a Christian is to become a
"look-alike" of Jesus Christ. The Father loves His Son *so*
much that He is determined to fill heaven with people
just like Him! Every day the Father is working in you to
make you more like His Son. All of life is meant to train
you for the day when you step into heaven and begin an
eternity of ruling and reigning with Jesus. You are in
"schooling for ruling" and in "training for reigning."
Your personal destiny is already fixed. You are *"predes-*
tined to be conformed to the likeness of His Son, that He might
be the firstborn of many brothers" (Rom. 8:29).

Imagine being one of these many brothers who will sit on the throne and reign forever with Jesus! But here's the incredible news:

Welcome to the Throne Room!

As a beloved child of God, you have been escorted into the throne room of heaven already. Grace has brought you home. As you pray to the Father, you are praying seated in heavenly places in Christ Jesus. Read this Scripture carefully; then read it again. Place it on the tablets of your heart.

> *God, who is rich in mercy, made us alive with Christ even when we were dead in transgressions... it is by grace you have been saved. And God RAISED US UP WITH CHRIST AND SEATED US WITH HIM in the heavenly realms in Christ Jesus.*
>
> Ephesians 2:4-6

You are an enthroned intercessor. In a sense, the Rapture has already happened for every believer. *"For through Him we both [Jew and Gentile] have ACCESS to the Father by one Spirit"* **(Eph. 2:18).** You are now one who has rights and privileges before the Father. Grace has fully gifted you to cry out and plead your case before the Father of Eternity. If God were to bless you any more and raise you up any higher, it would be a threat to the Trinity!! Every privilege that Jesus has, you have. The righteousness that Jesus has, you have. The position before the Father that Jesus has, you have. Got it? It's time for rejoicing!

There is a company of people in heaven that has been redeemed by the blood of the Lamb. They are the saints of God. You and I, we are enthroned intercessors who gaze on the glory and beauty of Jesus as we speak to Him in prayer. If you will begin to see yourself as already seated with Him in glory, your prayer life will never be the same.

Israel asked God to be an intercessor. Their faith was in His ability to come and rescue them. Listen to their plea: *"Awake, awake! Clothe Yourself with strength, O arm of the Lord; awake as in days gone by, as in generations of old"* (Isa. 51:9). But listen to the Lord's reply: *"Awake, awake, O ZION, clothe yourself with strength. Put on your garments of splendor...Shake off your dust (nature); rise up, sit enthroned!"* (Isa. 52:1-2).

God's answer is "It's time for *you* to awake and stir yourself. Take off the dust-man and put on the glory-garments. Rise to the place where you belong and sit at My side as we bring forth destiny to the earth" He is calling you to be an enthroned intercessor!

> But YOU HAVE COME to Mount Zion (God's Throne Room), to the heavenly Jerusalem, the city of the living God. You have come to thousands upon thousands of angels in joyful assembly...YOU HAVE COME to God, the Judge of all men...to Jesus the Mediator of a new covenant.
>
> Hebrews 12:22-24

"To him who overcomes, I will give the right to sit with me on my throne" (Rev. 3:21).

"Let the beloved of the Lord rest secure in Him, for He shields him (her) all day long, and the one the Lord loves rests between His shoulders" (Deut. 33:12).

Why the Devil Hates Intercessors

Simply stated, because *you* are a threat to his dark kingdom! Intercessors come under unusual attack from demonic powers because they are the ones doing some of the greatest damage to his strategies, his schemes, his web of deceit. It is important for every intercessor to flow under proper spiritual authority, but even so, you will get hit. As an enthroned intercessor *you* make the devil jealous.

In Isaiah 14:12-17, there is an account of one called the *"morning star, son of the dawn."* He had been cast down to the earth for his pride and rebellion. Scholars conclude this is a clear reference to Lucifer, the devil. Listen to what caused his fall:

> *You said in your heart, "I WILL ASCEND to heaven; I WILL RAISE MY THRONE above the stars of God; I WILL SIT ENTHRONED ON THE MOUNTAIN OF ASSEMBLY on the utmost heights of the sacred mountain. I WILL ASCEND above the tops of the clouds; I WILL MAKE MYSELF LIKE THE MOST HIGH."*

◈ He boasted that he would ascend—YOU have been seated on high!

◈ He boasted that his throne would be over all—YOU are invited to sin on Jesus' throne!

◈ He boasted that he would be on the sacred mountain—YOU are seated on MT. ZION!

◈ He boasted that he would ascend over the clouds—YOU are seated in the glory cloud!

◆ He boasted that he would be like the Most High — YOU will one day be LIKE CHRIST!

This is why the devil hates you! You have fulfilled his dreams! You have freely been given the place he sought after. It cost you nothing;grace has lifted you on high. He has been cast down. YOU have been freely and fully anointed with the Spirit of God and raised up to sit with Christ in the high places. Since he cannot touch God, he will come after you with jealous fury. Does that explain why it is a struggle for you to break through in prayer? But remember you are covered in the blood of the Lamb. Hidden in the high places, the devil can't even find you! Read Colossians 3:1-4.

The Jesus Stairway and His Ascending Angels

There are at least two clear references to the "Jesus stairway" in the Bible. The first is found in Genesis 28. Jacob was running away from his angry brother Esau. Having walked for two or three days, he was weary and exhausted as night fell. In the twilight he set up camp at Bethel. Some believe this was the ancient place where his grandfather, Abraham, years before had erected an altar to Yahweh (12:8). In his helpless, lonely condition, a new revelation would be given to Jacob. Stones for a pillow—heaven as a canopy above—the cold ground beneath, Jacob fell asleep and dreamed.

He saw a vision of the Almighty, and he heard the words of God. Jacob saw a stairway, a ladder reaching up to heaven. Upon this ladder, he saw angels ascending and descending. God Himself was at the top of this angel-filled stairway, speaking to him. What a mysterious sight this would have been to the frightened Jacob!

The second place we find a clear reference to this stairway to heaven is in the New Testament, John 1. Jesus Christ is clearly the ladder that reaches from earth (His human nature) to heaven (His heavenly nature). Jesus spoke to Nathaniel, using the same terminology—*"I tell you the truth, you shall see heaven open, and the angels of God ascending and descending upon the Son of Man" (John 1:51).* Jacob received the glorious revelation that Jesus is the stairway to heaven! It is when we see Him that the Father speaks to our hearts.

All of God's favors come to us on this Jesus-ladder. Jesus is the only valid entry into the spirit realm. He is the way into the heavenlies. This Jesus-ladder was filled with angels ascending and descending. Who are these angels?

Note the order. They ascended *first*. It does not say they were descending and ascending; which would be true if they were the angels of heaven. If you ascend first, you are leaving earth to go to heaven. Whoever these angels are, they ascend from the earth to heaven then descend back to the earth. These "angels" are intercessors, *promise-claimers.* There are angels that are *angels,* and there are angels that are *human.* The Greek word used in the New Testament for angels is merely *angelos* or "messengers." They can refer to people or to angels. Paul wrote to the Galatians and told them they had welcomed him in their midst as if he were an "angel" of God (Gal. 4:14). In Revelation 2-3, John is instructed to write to the seven churches and to the seven angels of those churches. Those angels were messengers or pastors[1] over those churches.

In the Old Testament, even Jesus, in His pre-incarnate form, appeared as the "Angel of the Lord." In Genesis 18:2 three angels come to Abraham and are described as "three men" (Gen. 19:1). Angels are also seen as the end-time reapers (Matt. 24:31). God's angels, *His messengers*, will be sent as fiery flames of revival into all the earth. From the ministry of angels (messengers), the great harvest will be brought in. Beloved, *we* are the angels that ascend and descend upon the Son of Man, the Jesus-ladder! We are the ascending Angels, the enthroned intercessors who go up through the open door (Rev. 4:1) and come down with authority to execute the will of God on the earth. This revelation given to Jacob was repeated by the Lord to Nathaniel.

Our friend Nathaniel had his eyes on the earth ("Can any good thing come out of Nazareth?"), but Jesus told him his eyes would see *heaven opened*. Jesus prophesied of an end time opened heaven that would allow access to the messengers of the Lord (intercessors) to go into the throne room by the blood of the Lamb and return with the strategies, wisdom, and glory of heaven. The Lord wants to cause you, His enthroned intercessor, to climb the Jesus stairway and release on earth what God has released in heaven!

Listen to the words of St. Germanus of Constantinople[2] as he spoke of this "ladder-climbing":

> *The souls of Christians are called to assemble with the prophets, apostles, and hierarchies in order to recline with Abraham, Isaac, and Jacob at the mystical banquet of the Kingdom of Christ. Thereby having come into the unity of faith and communion of the Spirit through the dispensation of the One who died for us and is sitting at the right hand of the Father, we are no longer on earth but standing by the royal Throne of God in heaven, where Christ is, just as He Himself says: "Righteous Father, sanctify in Your Name those whom You have me, so that where I am, they may be with Me."*

In the *Odes of Solomon* there are frequent references to ecstatic, visionary trips to paradise.[3] One example states, "I rested on the Spirit of the Lord, and She lifted me up to heaven."

End-time intercession must become an act of climbing the Jesus-ladder. We go up to the heavens with our cries for intervention; then we descend back to earth with the answer! Intercession is seeing heaven open and the messengers of God ascending and descending upon the Son of Man. It's time to go up, holy angels! It is time to let your heart-cry ascend until the promise descends. We need answers to our prayers. We must ascend the Hill of the Lord, the Jesus-ladder until He rains down His Spirit upon us. We *all* have access to the Father by one Spirit (Eph. 2:18). His door is open, and the stairway is available to *you*. Before you can climb, believe you are His angel, and believe that you can ascend.

The answers you need are not on the earth—they are in the throne room—and heaven is closer than you think. Perhaps this is the ascending "highway" spoken of by the prophet Isaiah? (Isa. 35:8-9, 57:14-15, 62:10).

Hello, angel. Did you go to heaven today? Did you ascend and get the will of God for today? Did you bring it back and execute it? Are you on the stairway today? Climb that Jesus-ladder and find the fulfillment of your covenant promises, just as Jacob did. God says, *"You have to come where I live to get what you need. You have access to the heavenlies. I left the door open and the lights on. Come up, you mighty angels and praise the Lord for His mighty works."* Answers to prayer will be found when we ascend with the request and return in faith with the promise ful-filled. This is the "hidden way of the stairs," the hiding places on the mountainside of the Lord (Song of Songs 2:14).

What would God tell Jacob at the top of this ladder? What would God tell us if we were to climb Jacob's Ladder? Would He scold Jacob for being a crafty deceiver? Would He rebuke him for his lack of faith? Perhaps God will just strike him dead for all the rotten things he has done. No, He reveals Himself to Jacob as the One who will never leave or forsake Him.

A revelation of grace—a stream of assurances washes over wayward Jacob! And so, God spoke His affirmation and renewed His blessing to all the "ascending" ones in these last days. Be bold, you angel! Go up that stairway and find the destiny and purpose of your life. Go up the Jesus stairway higher into that place where He has already seated you as an intercessor. A Bride at His side! Enthroned intercessors will be those violent ones who take the kingdom by force. With the anointing and zeal of John the Baptist, they will not be held back by those who tell them what they cannot do. Go up, O you mighty ones, you angels of the Lord who do His bidding (Ps. 29). Until you become the "voice of the Lord" to the nations (waters) of the earth!

Filling the Prayer Bowl

God will pour out upon the earth what is in one of two bowls. One is a bowl of wrath; the other is a bowl of intercession. There is a bowl filled with judgments and wrath that is about to be poured upon the earth: *"In the hand of the Lord is a cup full of foaming wine mixed with spices; He pours it out, and all the wicked of the earth drink it down to its very dregs" (Ps. 75:8).* This cup of fermenting wine is a picture of the combined generational sins and the wickedness of nations. When their cup is full of iniquity, wrath is poured out on earth. But there is another bowl, a cup of prayer that the Church must begin to fill:

"...the twenty-four elders fell down before the Lamb. Each one had a harp [worship] and they were holding golden bowls full of incense, which are the prayers of the saints"(Rev. 5:8).

"Another angel [messenger], who had a golden censer [utensil], came and stood at the altar. He was given much incense to offer, with the prayers of all the saints, on the golden altar before the throne" (Rev. 8:3-4).

Every time the saints gather to intercede, the golden bowl of intercession begins to fill. As this bowl runs over and is poured out, revival power flows. God waits until one of these two bowls is full before He picks it up in His hand and pours it out. Every church has a bowl to fill. Are you actively filling your cup of intercession? Your prayers are a sweet incense to Jesus. Let Him inhale your intercession!

Ezekiel's Vision and the Fiery Cherubim

Ezekiel was a visionary prophet. He saw the heavens opened (like Jacob, Nathaniel, and John) Ezekiel 1 reads better than a Frank Perretti novel and has better graphics than a Steven Spielberg movie. It is spellbinding!

Ezekiel 1:1 reads, **"In the thirtieth year** [when he was 30]....**the heavens were opened and I saw visions of God."** Ezekiel was both a prophet and a priest (Ezek. 1:2). Every priest who joined the temple priesthood had to wait until he was thirty. When they turned thirty, they were inducted into the priesthood (Num. 4:3). This was to be the year Ezekiel began his ministry as a priest, but something prevented it. They were in exile. There was no temple, no ministry to perform. Ezekiel was denied the opportunity that every priest dreamed about—coming before the Lord in the Temple to worship the Lord. But God had other plans for this priest. He was going to anoint him as a prophet instead.

Ezekiel began his prophetic ministry as a watchman at the age of thirty (Ezek. 3:17). The separated priest became the anointed prophet to Israel. *Ezekiel had a throne room encounter*, as an enthroned intercessor. By the River Kebar (the river of long ago — the river of revelation knowledge that God has kept from eternity), the divine hand of the Lord came upon Ezekiel and anointed him as a prophet.

Immediately he was taken into the Spirit realm and saw an immense windstorm—a whirlwind of divine activity, a hurricane of holiness, a tempest of truth. What a vision this was, this glowing, flashing, twisting pillar of cloud and fire. How would one come into that whirlwind and survive? It was a wind and fire, a spiritual volcano. Before Ezekiel's eyes he saw spinning forth the lava of glory.

As he gazed upon this pillar of fire, he saw four living creatures walking in the fire. Nebuchadnezzar saw four "men" in a different fire (Dan. 3:25). These living creatures all looked in appearance and in their form as men (Ezek. 1:5). The living creatures that Ezekiel saw were like men—**intercessors in the fire!**

Scholars conclude that Ezekiel's living creatures were in fact "cherubim." They become a spiritual picture of the man who stands before God, the Lord Jesus Christ. With a face on each side, Jesus is seen differently in all four gospels. They have a face of a man, a lion, an ox, and an eagle. Each of these represent the four-fold nature of the Man Christ Jesus. YET they also represent the ministry of Jesus before the throne, our Magnificent Intercessor. As one with Him, as enthroned intercessors, we are to join in partnership with Jesus and become the fiery cherubim with wings touching one another and flying in perfect unity.

Intercessors, it's time to touch wings! As you link arms (or wings) with others and network together with the prayer partners of Jesus, the glory storm will come over our land.

What about these wheels? What are they? And what does it mean that the spirit of the living creatures was in the wheels? I believe these spinning wheels speak of three things:

1. The spinning wheels of God are *generators* of power. I see the wheels spinning as the saints pray on earth. More prayer, more power released. It is the prayers of the saints that cause the wheels to spin.

2. These wheels within wheels are like heavenly *gyroscopes* of glory that turn as we intercede. Our place is before the Father showing our faces to Him and crying out for the whirlwind of divine activity to stir the hearts of men in worship and surrender to God.

3. The wheels also speak of *government*. God's kingdom is in motion as it comes to the earth. The throne of God sits on wheels (Dan. 7:9). The governmental throne of the universe sits on spinning wheels of glory. God governs on top of these wheels.

If you look at the earth's rotation around the sun, you see an example of a spinning wheel within a spinning wheel. As the earth spins, it rotates around the spinning sun. This is how God created His universe to operate—all of it spinning around His throne as His redeemed ones (living creatures) pray on the crystal pavement.

A wheel does not move by itself. It must be pushed, pulled, or driven. There must be a power or force that causes the wheels to spin. Ezekiel's vision was of the "spirit of the living creatures," which caused the wheels to turn. It was as though the living creatures themselves were the ones exerting the power to cause the wheels to roll. They moved by spirit-power.

> *When the creatures moved, they [the wheels] also moved; when the creatures stood still, they also stood still; and when the creatures rose from the ground, the wheels rose along with them, because the spirit of the living creatures was in the wheels.*
>
> Ezekiel 1:21

The government of God (His throne set on wheels) moves as the living creatures (intercessors) flow as one in the power of the Spirit of God within them. As they rise up in intercession, the wheels of God also rise up along with them. The partnership of heaven and earth begins to happen.

The wheels with *rainbow rims* were high, wheels within wheels. And spread out over the heads of the creatures was an expanse, a pavement like sapphire, sparkling like ice. Think about that for a moment. You stand upon this place when you offer your prayers to Him. It is like a great sea of glass mingled with fire, a sparkling sapphire pavement clear as crystal with fire flashing upon it (Rev. 4:6 and 15:2).

And those *rushing wings* of the cherubim! They are so powerful it sounds like an army, like the voice of the Lord. These cherubim stirred up the winds as they rode the wheels. Do you get the picture? Do you understand where you are as you cry out for God's power to move?

"*The appearance of the living creatures was like burning coals of fire or like torches. Fire moved back and forth among the creatures; it was bright, and lightning flashed out of it. The creatures sped back and forth like flashes of lightning"* (Ezek. 1:13-14).

The Lord's living ones are like lightning flashing. They are executing warfare orders from their Commanding Officer. Like John the Baptist, you can become a burning and shining torch, with the lightning of God flashing in you!

Look again at what Ezekiel saw: a whirlwind, a rainbow of glory, the jasper throne, the sapphire pavement, cherubim, the mushroom cloud of His presence, flashing lightning, spirit beings beneath the throne surrounded by brilliant light, the center of the fire looking like glowing metal, the amber glow of the radiance of God, sparkling wheels. Does this make prayer a little more exciting for you? How can you be bored in a prayer meeting when you see yourself before this heavenly whirlwind? You cannot help but be overwhelmed! You enter this scene every time you come to prayer before God. WHAT AN ADVENTURE!

Perhaps the words of the apostle John will help us: *"There before me was a throne."* The rainbow of promise encircles you as you stand before this Throne. If you look closely, you can tell that every saint has a crown of gold on his head. We are enthroned intercessors with a golden crown upon our heads. What an honor God has bestowed upon us! Is this the scene you picture as you pray? Or do you still think God doesn't hear and prayer meetings are boring?

Do you realize that if suddenly you saw an open vision like what Ezekiel and John saw with the flashes of lightning, the sounds of thunder and wind—do you realize how you would quiver and shake and fall at His feet? The energy unleashed by your prayers, the powerful answers from the throne, are like rumblings of thunder as God issues His decrees!

Every time you pray, you come to the throne of God. Every time we lift our hearts toward God in prayer, an angel takes the incense in his hand, mixes it with fire from the altar of heaven, and flings it back to the earth. As this fire enters the atmosphere of earth, it creates a shock wave of power and becomes spiritual thunder. This should give us encouragement to pray!

We are not praying to be heard by the people around us. We are coming to Mt. Zion, the Mediator of a better covenant, every time we pray and do not even realize it. We have the glorious privilege of standing before the blazing splendor of Jesus on a "sea of glass." In His radiance we come to speak with the Creator of the Universe. The angels cry, "holy"; the more they say it, the more they see; the more they see, the more they say it. What would you say if you saw His glory? God invites you to pass through the mushroom cloud of Holy smoke—past the sapphire pavement, past the spinning sparkling wheels, past the rainbow, the flashing of lightning, the peals of thunder—and *participate in the purposes of God.*

We are kingdom officials who come to ask for divine intervention! Your intercession must be seen as urgent kingdom business. It gets better: he is King of kings, right? Well, who are the kings? We are a royal priesthood, you and I are the kings and priests (Rev. 1:6, 5:10). We intercede to One who reigns over kings. How is that for helping with an identity crisis? This King invites us to His throne and washes us in love. Enthroned with Him as kings to intercede! In Genesis 2, God made man lord over the earth with the power to take dominion and exercise authority over every living thing. He is Lord of lords!

Jesus wants to be the amen to your prayer (Rev. 3:14). Join Him as one of His enthroned intercessors, made to breathe together with Jesus. You will influence destiny every time you pray. Approach Him with faith, courage, and boldness—by the power of the blood of Jesus. Wisdom, grace, and strategies are released at the throne room. The answers we need are not on earth; they are in heaven. His wheels spin in response to our prayers. You can abandon your life to prayer when you get a glimpse of this!

**But you have come to Mount Zion,
to the heavenly Jerusalem,
the city of the living God.
You have come to thousands upon thousands
of angels in joyful assembly,
to the church of the firstborn,
whose names are written in heaven.
You have come to God, the judge of all men,
to the spirits of righteous men made perfect,
to Jesus the mediator of a new covenant.**

Hebrews 12:22-24

---

[1] *Strongs Concordance* gives the word "pastor" as a possible translation.
[2] St. Germanus of Constantinople, *On the Divine Liturgy*, trans. Paul Meyendorff (Crestwood, NY: St Vladimir's Seminary Press, 1984), p. 101.
[3] Aune, *Prophecy in Early Christianity*, p. 287.

The Sons of Issachar

Men of Issachar, Who understood the times
And knew what Israel should do — 200 chiefs,
With all their relatives under their command.
I Chronicles 12:32

The birth of intercession signals the end of spiritual barrenness in our land. As God prepares the earth for the mega-move of His Spirit, He first raises us a company of intercessors who understand the times and seasons. The recent emergence of the world-wide intercessory movement has been a breath of fresh air. No longer are intercessors marginalized; they have become increasingly recognized as God's "shock troops", who will pull down long resistant strongholds. It is crucial that we become prayer partners with Jesus. We must labor with Him in prayer to escort the will of God to the earth.

Intercession brings the future into the present. Intercessors see something coming prophetically with the eye of faith. Then by fervent prayer, fasting, worship, and intercession they bring the vision into present day reality. Intercession, is like a vital tributary that feeds into a prophetic river, giving the river substance and cutting power. This river carries the purposes of God into the sea of fulfillment at its proper point. Without intercession, God's purposes on earth may be hindered, even postponed. The future belongs to intercessors. We must become prayer partners with Jesus!

Daniel operated both in the role of prophet and intercessor. He understood the written prophecies of the number of years of Israel's captivity. With prophetic revelation from visions, angelic visitations, and insights from the Word, he understood the times perfectly. His prayer of intercession in Daniel 9 escorted the will of God to the earth and the prophecy was fulfilled.

Ezra walked in the anointing of priest and intercessor. With prayer, fasting, and intercession Ezra ascertained the timing of God through the writings of Jeremiah and greatly influenced the nation by his prayers (Ezra 9). Nehemiah also, knew the time had come to repair the walls of Jerusalem, and despite being a solitary cup bearer, he went before the king (intercession) and pleaded Israel's case (Neh. 1).

Queen Esther fasted for three days, then boldly went before the king (intercession) at her own peril, to plead for Israel (Esther 4:16). Daniel, Ezra, Nehemiah, Esther all influenced a nation. When intercessors arise, nations will be changed. As we enter the 21st century, true intercessors must be restored in every nation.

Who were the Sons of Issachar? They were the smallest, least mentioned tribe in the Bible. They were not dominant or prestigious like Judah from which King David and our Lord Jesus Christ came. They were not prosperous like Ephraim, which boasted leaders like Joshua and Samuel. They were not the strong tribe like Dan, which produced a Samson. They were not a special tribe like Levi, the priestly one. They had no great history. They were nobodies.

So why did God in I Chronicles 12:32 point to them as a people so crucial in Israel's history? If we understand the keys, we will understand the intercessory movement.

This cryptic prophecy will soon become a rallying cry in the Church as we begin to recognize a new breed of prophetic Intercessors arising among the nations—they will be known as the Sons of Issachar!

"Of the Sons of Issachar, who understood the times and knew what Israel should do - 200 chiefs, with all their relatives under their command" (I Chronicles 12:32).

I Chronicles 12 gives a list of all the various tribes of Israel that pledged their support to David. The defection had begun. These tribes were the army divisions equipped for war, to turn the kingdom of Saul over to David (I Chron. 12:23-38). With the exception of one small tribe, all the others were made up of very large numbers —averaging thousands or tens of thousands. Only the men of Issachar numbered so few—200!

Notice they knew what the signs meant prophetically, and they knew where God wanted to take the nation. They were not mighty in numbers, but they were mighty in their spirits—men of unusual understanding and discernment! They were all united in one thing: influence. They were all chiefs who had others under their influence. They were a company of 200 chiefs who influenced the nation far beyond anyone would expect from their numbers! Are today's intercessors the fulfillment of the Sons of Issachar? Five things about them must be understood in the light of this pre-revival, world-wide intercessory prayer movement:

Birthed by God as a Sign (Genesis 30:17-18)

The Sons of Issachar are birthed by God as a sign that spiritual barrenness is over. A new season of fertility, prosperity, and blessing will come with the birth of the Sons of Issachar. Issachar was the son of Jacob and Leah. Jacob married two wives, Rachel and Leah, who were sisters. Imagine that! Tricked by Laban, their father, into marrying Leah first, Jacob had to work seven years before he could take Rachel's hand in marriage. He really loved Rachel more that Leah. However, in terms of bearing children, Leah was the far more fertile. When the Lord saw that Leah was unloved, He opened her womb, but Rachel was barren. Leah brought forth four sons for Jacob —Reuben, Simeon, Levi, and Judah. Then the strangest thing happened. God shut her womb and she stopped bearing children (Gen. 29:30-32).

Leah was not loved; Rachel was dearly loved. Leah had children; Rachel had none. One felt superior (because of her sons), and the other felt inferior. There was fighting and division in Jacob's household. Rachel decided to look for another way of solving her problem of barrenness. She took her maid, Bilhah, and gave her to Jacob to be her surrogate (Gen. 30:3). Now we have three women running the house! That could mean only one thing—more strife! Abraham and Sarah's compromise was now passed on to another generation.

Bilhah conceived twice and bore Jacob two sons, Dan and Naphtali. When Leah saw this, she got in on the act and gave her maid, Zilpah, to Jacob (Gen. 30:9-13). Zilpah bore Jacob two more sons, Gad and Asher. Now Jacob had *eight* sons. But Rachel's womb was still silent, and Leah's womb had been closed for years. Strife and barrenness were in the house! To attempt to remedy the barrenness, Reuben, Leah's eldest, went into the fields and brought home to mother some mandrakes (Gen. 30:14-15). (Mandrakes were highly prized in that society as a fertility herb.) Reuben was using worldly methods to attempt to end the strife of barrenness.

But here's the problem: Jacob slept with Rachel, not Leah. Leah sold the mandrakes to Rachel in exchange for the one thing that really mattered to her, a night of intimacy with Jacob. From that encounter, Issachar was miraculously born! God opened her womb after more than twelve years of barrenness! Genesis 30:17 says that God listened to Leah. Rachel wanted mandrakes; Leah wanted God's miracle. Issachar was birthed by God through prayer as a sign that barrenness was over. She produced other children after this night; her barrenness and strife had ended. The birth of the Sons of Issachar heralds the beginning of a work of God in answer to prayer. The name Issachar means "reward!"

The intercessory prayer movement is the result of forerunners, those who prayed while pastors and workers were busy building big churches and programs. They were the ones who prayed while the Bible teachers were learning Greek and Hebrew. But God has heard these Leahs as forerunners of the intercessory prayer movement. They prayed for the Sons of Issachar to come forth. Now this movement is out of control!

Birthed to Be Burden, Bearers (Genesis 49:14-15)

In Genesis 49 Jacob blessed his sons before his death. These blessings were powerful prophetic statements as to their destiny. When Jacob turned to bless Issachar, he said, *"Issachar is a strong donkey, lying down between two burdens; he saw that rest was good, and that the land was pleasant; he bowed his shoulder to bear a burden..."* (NKJV).

The Sons of Issachar are donkeys! They are burden bearers. A horse loves speed, a donkey is made for carrying burdens. A donkey is focused and sure-footed when it walks on mountain heights. A horse needs blinders or things will easily distract, but a donkey keeps its attention on the trail ahead. A donkey can endure weeks of hard conditions with little rest. Sound like an intercessor?

The other sons were blessed for what they were to do—only Issachar was blessed for what he *saw*: *"Issachar SAW that rest was good and that the land was pleasant...."* The Hebrew word here for "rest" can mean both physical and spiritual rest. There is an anointing of rest for those who give their lives in intercession. Regardless of the shaking of the nations, intercessors can rest in the intimate presence of God. Nothing will shake their confidence, for they have entered into His rest (Heb. 3:11).

Issachar, the donkey, saw that rest was good. Nobody else did. He saw the anointing of rest. Burdens must be carried but from the pleasant land of resting in God's sweet presence. We must bow our shoulders to the burden of the Lord. God has a burden to share, but He waits for intercessors to find the resting place and will bow their shoulder to His burden. True Sons of Issachar submit to voluntary labor and become slaves to prayer! Issachar bore it because he could see in the Spirit what God wanted to do in the land. God offers to His intercessors, His friends, the opportunity to partner with Him to bring these things to pass. He is looking for those whom He can trust with His burdens.

Easily misunderstood by leaders, these Sons of Issachar of today often find themselves shut in with God with burdens they cannot explain. God is praying through them. God is sharing His secrets with them. How can you describe to others the burdens of God? These intercessors need room to grow. The shepherds must feed them as the Word of God will be their strength.

Intercessors must be led carefully, for they willingly carry heavy burdens. We must remember that it was the donkey that carried Jesus into Jerusalem. Could it be that the intercessors are those whom God has chosen to "carry" His presence into the nations? We are to loose them, for the Master has need of intercessors. We have never yet ridden the donkey of intercession to see how far we can go in believing prayer. There are many adventures awaiting those brave warriors who long to ride the wheels of God. Go for it!

Birthed for Unique Spiritual Warfare (Judges 5:15)

Before an invasion can take place, the "shock troops" must loosen up enemy territory. This "prayer barrage" totally demoralizes the enemy and places the invasion forces at a great advantage. These shock troops often carry the most aggressive firepower. Intercessors are God's shock troops who were born for battle! They are called to precede the final invasion forces. These Sons of Issachar are birthed to engage in a unique form of warfare.

In Judges 4 and 5, we see Israel under the oppressive rule of a king named Jabin, who had a commander called Sisera. Their troops were numerous with an army of 900 iron chariots. They were like armored tank divisions of today. The prophetess Deborah was called to be a deliverer, a Judge of Israel. She often sat under a palm tree (symbol of victory) until prophetic vision and the word of the Lord guided her. She sent for Barak, a leader in Israel, to come and lead God's people into battle. Barak balked; he was not a man of war. He told Deborah if she went with him into battle, he would go.

Left with little choice, Deborah went with Barak into the battlefield. Together they came against Jabin and won a famous victory. Sisera, the commander, fled by foot and was killed by a woman after going into a tent to rest. Here's how the battle was won. God sent a flood to the Kishon River valley. As the river flooded, the wheels of the chariots got stuck in the mud and became useless.

Without the chariot divisions, Barak easily conquered the troops as God won the victory that day.

So what role did Issachar play? Five tribes refused to go into battle. Of those who entered the fray, it was the Princes of Issachar who went against the iron chariots with Deborah and Barak (Judges 5:15). This is a picture of the *prophetic* and *intercession* flowing together to conquer spiritual foes. First in, first to behold the miracles!

The Sons of Issachar came in first as the shock troops. They gambled everything. They just had to win. Led by a woman, against insurmountable odds, the Sons of Issachar charged forth under prophetic covering. They knew this was the time; this was the hour for victory— they could smell it! Born for battle, they went in where five warrior tribes dared to enter! Their reward? They saw with their eyes the intervention of God! The flooding river won the battle. With the enemy trapped in the mud, they saw how God fights the battle.

Investing your life in intercession is a gamble you can't lose. God gives to you the privilege of seeing first-hand the fulfillment of purpose and destiny. You have prayed for it; you will see it! In today's world there are many of the WRONG type of gamblers. They fill casinos and go broke buying lotto tickets. Against hopeless odds they do not give up; they keep throwing their money into the slots in the illusion that the big one is just around the corner.

Where are the gamblers for God? They are the intercessors who are prepared to enter high level spiritual battles. They march in where others fear to tread. They are the first to reap. They went in first, so they will be blessed first. Intercession is the gamble you cannot lose!

Many today do not understand the power and purpose of intercessory prayer meetings. They are like the tribes who didn't want to get involved. Just because you don't want to fight doesn't mean there is no battle going on! Intercessors are those who are willing to pay the price to be at the forefront of the battle scene. They don't treat fasting lightly. Mention prayer and they drop to their knees to pray—ready for battle.

Birthed to Be Led
(The Issachar/Judah Anointing)

Intercessors always function better under authority. They are born to be a submitted people. If they want the anointing to be continual and abundant, they need proper oversight. If they are to command the demons in the heavenlies, they must be a submitted people. The dilemma of pastors and leaders is often "What do I do with these intercessors? They are almost a law unto themselves?" Here's the answer:

Down deep, every intercessor craves to be connected to leadership. Pastors default their calling when they fail to take them under their wing and provide adequate leadership for them. Many pastors feel intimidated by those who seem to spend so much time in prayer (often more than they do!). But criticism or defaulting the leadership is not the answer. They must be led. Guide them, showing godly authority over their fragile spirits, and a divine partnership will develop. If leaders fail in this, the intercessory movement that is touching your church may soon fizzle or spin out of orbit with the vision of the leadership.

As hard as it is to swallow, intercessors *sense more* of what is going on in the spirit compared to some leaders. They are wired this way. They may miss it, but with pastoral direction those 200 chiefs will bring insight and focus to many ministries. Pastors, do not discount the input of your intercessors. Just because their personal backgrounds may not make them leadership material, do not overlook them. Wise is the pastor who identifies their calling, nurtures their gift and leads them. They were born to be beside YOU!

One of the greatest ways a pastor can encourage an intercessor is to remain connected with them, valuing their gifts and bringing direction where there is a need. Knowing their pastor is behind them is like a booster rocket to their prayer life! It helps them immensely to know their pastor or leader is willing to listen to them even if they may be misled. Often, they are seeking our correction or adjustment.

Although the Sons of Issachar saw the times, discerned them, and knew what Israel was to do, they never led the nation. Their anointing was released when they walked in the yoke with leadership. This is seen with Deborah, with David, and with Judah.

In Genesis 49:11 Jacob's blessing for Judah was that he would have a DONKEY. The donkey belonged to Judah. Issachar was to be led by Judah. The Sons of Issachar do not operate on their own authority, but their anointing grows as they are submitted to God's delegated authority. Their task was simply to follow the leader!

Judah was the tribe that led Israel in their marches. Judah was not the eldest son of Jacob, but he was the one, God had given the authority. Israel's king was to be born of Judah. By far, Judah was the pre-eminent tribe of Israel. God also ordained that the tribes be paired up in a specific order. Guess which tribe was always paired up with the leadership tribe?

Issachar was promoted next to Judah, the tribe with the authority. Issachar was ninth in line but was placed next to Judah. That is God's order. Intercessors must walk under the shadow of the anointing to be fulfilled and powerful (Num. 7:12-17). Next to Judah,

Issachar was the tribe nearest the glory. As the cloud of Glory led Israel, it was Judah, then Issachar (Num. 1:1-14). In Deuteronomy 27 and 28, when the blessings were handed out to Israel's tribes, it was Issachar standing next to Judah.

When intercessors move under authority, they move into the realm of glory in God's presence. Nowhere in Scripture do we see the Sons of Issachar leading the way. They influence, they move the heart of God, but they walk under authority. "Judah" means "praise." As intercessors move under anointed praises, fresh revelation is unlocked to them.

We repeat: Intercessors have an anointing that grows with submission! If you are becoming a prayer-partner with Jesus, you must understand this. If you move outside of the authority of God for your church, your impact as an intercessor is finished. The role of a pastor is to bring a God-ordained covering of protection and wisdom to the intercessor.

God has given authority over us to keep us on track, focused, refreshed. Leaders release vision and direction. Placed by God, they are to flow with His heart, keeping the big picture in view. Often intercessors confuse their role, their revelation, with the bigger picture. As an intercessor, you are called support and carry the vision of the pastor or primary leader. You are not called to change your pastor. You are called to support him or her.

The role of pastor and intercessor is like two police officers working on a beat together. One provides the prayer cover as the other has the authority to break the door down! Be sure to value partnering in Kingdom duties. Working together, the Church advances. We all contribute something, but it is God's leaders who provide the tracks for us to run on. When we get off track, we lose momentum and end up sitting on the sideline. Intercessors are birthed to be led. They function best when honored by leadership. We must see the ministry of intercession maximized so that God's wheels will spin, releasing destiny on earth.

Birthed to Tap into Revival (II Chronicles 30:1-18)

Intercessors are birthed to be spiritual revivalists. They can smell revival. Every revival in history can be traced back to someone or to groups of people who took hold of the hem of His garment and would not let Him go until the Spirit is poured out. They await the awakening.

II Chronicles 30 gives the account of a wonderful time of revival in Israel's history under the reign of Hezekiah. The king cleansed the temple and brought back true worship. He destroyed the idols. He made provision for the priests to sanctify themselves. He restored the feasts and sacrifices. The Feast of Passover had not been observed as a unified nation since the days of Solomon. All of this happened quite suddenly (II Chron. 29:36). All at once revival came. The priests were performing their functions, sacrifices were offered in the midst of anointed worship. There was a joining of repentance and rejoicing.

So it is with revival. It will catch many by surprise. But did it catch the Sons of Issachar by surprise? Hezekiah had sent out an invitation to all of Israel to return to the Lord. The Temple doors were opened. "Come and let us worship as one and restore the sacrifices!" Messengers were sent all throughout the land to herald this call. Everywhere the runners went, people laughed and mocked at them. They had become too secular. "What? Go back to the sacrifices and Temple worship? You gotta be kidding!"

Despite the ridicule, a small remnant from Asher, Manasseh, and Zebulun humbled themselves and came to Jerusalem to keep the Passover. *But make way for Issachar* With no mention that they were invited—out of nowhere—Issachar appeared! No mention is given that the king's runners had informed Issachar. Perhaps they were ignored because they were so few in number. They just showed up! They could smell revival. They knew a move of God was underfoot. Intercessors are like that. They crash the party. They do not wait to be invited; spiritual revivalists just show up!

They actually were so hungry for revival that the Sons of Issachar started eating and celebrating the Passover even though they had not yet purified themselves. Hezekiah (leadership) prayed for them, and God overlooked their sin and healed them. (Hunger for God gets away with some things!)

Today's Sons of Issachar tap into the burdens of God for revival and intercede for it long before others do. Bees smell honey; intercessors smell revival. They are quick to recognize the fresh initiatives of the Spirit and are quick to interpret them, even if it is still in its infancy (e.g., Anna in Luke 2). Join the Sons of Issachar, and you will see the spiritual world! Be ready, you praying ones. REVIVAL is on the way. Sweet mercies are falling from heaven. *Make way for the sons of Issachar!*

Calling All Intercessors!

You are not an elite group, no more special than any other in the Body of Christ. But you do have a particular calling and burden. You must be diligent to become that prayer partner that Jesus is looking for. May His eyes gaze upon YOU and find your heart, a manger—a place where He gives birth to eternal purpose.

Walk with victorious insight. Join Jesus in His triumph over every dark power. His cross is your Torch of Truth. Take it to the streets. Let others know that Jesus has won every battle and leads YOU in one continual triumph (II Cor. 2:14). Who are those who take the Kingdom by force? Those who storm the Citadel of God and bring the future into the present? Who are those who know firsthand the miracle power of God? *THE SONS OF ISSACHAR!*

YOU are God's burden bearer. You were birthed to signal an end to barrenness. You must become one of God's shock troops, gamblers for God! As you submit to God's delegated authority, YOU will be a channel for the River. You will be a pointer to spiritual revival in your land. Be faithful, Ye sons of Issachar! *Destiny awaits you. Grace will empower you!* Your true resting place is leaning on Him!

Lesson Eleven

Prayer Partners with Jesus

❖ ❖ ❖ ❖ ❖

The highest heavens belong to the LORD,
But the earth he has given to man.
Psalm 115:16

Promotion is coming to the Body of Christ. Our Lord Jesus is going to prepare His Bride for reigning with Him forever. Our Bridegroom-King is about to include His Bride in the governmental affairs of His universe. As we labor alongside of the Son of God in prayer, we become His "help-mate" in fulfilling the Father's will for planet earth. It is a great mystery: Jesus wants us to share His throne! Yet we have so much more to learn.

God has given the dominion of the earth to mankind. Adam and Eve were entrusted with the affairs of earth and were created to be God's agents, His holy governors of the planet. This right to rule was forfeited when mankind fell into the darkness of selfish pride and independence. Yet the plan of heaven has not changed. The Father of Lights is still seeking men and women to rule with Him.

Jesus holds the title deed of the universe in His hands, and as His body on earth, we become His hands. As His covenant partner, His co-heir, WE HAVE HIS LIFE in us, sharers of one common life. As His life branches out through us – as the Branch Man springs up in us and buds with new life, the government and rulership of the earth will incrementally be given back to the passionate Bride.

The more we become like Him, the more we will do the works He has destined the Church to do (John 14:12). The goal of our life must be more than having a ministry; we must be able to say, "For to me, to live is Christ and to die is gain" (Phil. 1:21). Remember this: God loves His Son SO much, He is determined to fill heaven and earth with people just like Him.

◈ You are not just a human being on your way to heaven. You are a duplicate of the Son of God having an earthly experience!

◈ Life is O.J.T. (on-the-job-training) for ruling one day over the universe. You are in schooling for ruling and training for reigning! Earth's workshop will finish your preparation to sit on the throne with Jesus Christ, ruling over angels and nations—forever!

◈ The spirit of prayer will one day fall upon you and change you into another person. Living prayer, walking prayer, night and day prayer is coming to a church near you!

The Spirit of Prayer

The Holy Spirit has come to teach us to pray. Whenever you yield to Him or make room for Him and obey Him even a little, He leads you to prayer. The life within you in a life of prayer. The Holy Spirit prays. He knows what to pray and waits to be your personal prayer mentor. Does the Holy Spirit have room in you to lead you to pray?

Two spirits are flowing through one another. As you have fellowship with God, the Holy Spirit flows through you. As the Spirit of prayer fills you, all that you are starts to flow through HIM. Two spirits are flowing through one another; the greater the flow, the more prayer you have! This Holy Spirit is interceding and partnering with us as we pray in Him (Rom. 8:26-27).

The Spirit of Prayer is like a law of prayer. Whenever we live in the spirit, prayer rises from within. We move with God and God moves with us. Heaven's heart is not fulfilled until it is flowing through you. The prayers that move heaven are not released until they come from you. The spirit of prayer is what God wants to place upon His Church, making us prayer partners with the Lamb.

Elijah prayed through the Spirit of Prayer. Even though he was a man with similar problems and passions as any other, he prayed and the heavens closed. He prayed again, and the heavens opened. Elijah cooperated and flowed with the Spirit of Prayer.

"He prayed earnestly" (James 5:17). What this literally says is that Elijah "prayed with prayer" or "prayed in prayer." As he prayed, true prayer in the Spirit came forth. He prayed but the Spirit prayed through Him. Elijah became a prayer partner with the Spirit within him. They breathed together the same request. This type of prayer in prayer must come forth for the Church to move into the season of the open heavens.

Real prayer will cause us to be mingled with God. We will become a person of two parties; God mingled with us. Our spirit and the Spirit of Prayer join as one and enter heaven with a request that will be answered. This type of prayer expresses God Himself, not just His will. God's very life comes flowing through us as we pray to the Father. When He prays, you pray with Him. When you pray, God prays with you. He is one with you inside and out! In this prayer moment, you and God cannot be separated, for you are mingled as one.

As friends of God, we should be able to complete one another's sentences as we kneel with Jesus to pray with Him as His partner. We know each other that well! Let Him whisper His thoughts into you as you pray.

This is what both Paul and Jude call "praying in the Holy Spirit."[1] Both the spirit of the intercessor and the Spirit of God cry to the Father for an answer. This God-Man prayer combo is what the universe has waited for. God must take His fullness into man and through man to fill all things in every way (Eph. 1:22-23). Man must become the container of God and join eternity in the divine symphony of prayer on the sea of glass before the throne.

Almighty and Sons, Inc.

Your Father has included you in His company. It is a construction company. He is the senior partner, but since you are His child, He has included you as a co-signer to all the legal work required in running the business (ruling over the nations). God's plan is to partner with you as a Helpmate of Jesus Christ. There are certain things we must do as part of this partnership of **Almighty and Sons**. There are some things God will not do for us.

We must be the ones to pray, to fast, to give generously, to evangelize, to study the Word of God, to love our spouse and children, to go to the unreached tribes, to serve our local church, to develop a rich devotional life in God—all of these things are waiting OUR activity, our doing. It is not God's job to do these things for us. These are the secrets and mysteries of God.

Paul was one who devoted himself to the grace of God. He understood that it was God plus nothing. Yet, he refused to let grace be wasted on an undisciplined life. He labored in the grace of God. He worked in the energy of grace to become a follower of the Lamb in all things. But when it was all said and done,he knew it was only by the grace of God that he accomplished anything. Listen to his heart: *"But by the grace of God I am what I am, and His grace to me was not without effect. No, I worked harder than all of them – yet not I, but the grace of God that was with me"* (I Cor. 15:10). Grace works hard. Grace gives us strength to finish. Grace gives us the power to partner with divine energy. God works in us both to want and to finish His will, but we still have to work out our practical salvation day by day (Phil. 2:12-13).

God does not promote people with potential; He promotes people who are faithful. We look for qualifications; God looks for faithfulness. Matthew 25:23 teaches us that the Lord will say to His trustworthy ones: "Good and faithful servant" not "Good and *qualified* servant." The Lord grooms us and prepares us by giving us a small measure of responsibility and sees how we handle the problems and pressures. He sees if we will be faithful before He gives us more. Wherever the Lord has promoted someone, there you will find a faithful man/woman.

Between you call and your destiny, there is only one thing required—faithfulness (II Cor. 4:1-2). *The timing depends on you!* If you will be faithful, in time you will be honored by *God and men.* You may be anointed and blessed with gifts oozing out your pores, but if you are not faithful in the little things of life, you will be passed over. Faithful people are like corks. If you hold down, they will pop up! The tortoise always wins. The tortoise becomes an eagle; it grows wings and flies! Read Isaiah 40:30-31.

The Divine Partnership

God has chosen to adapt His intentions and deeds through this interaction with us called prayer. Prayer moves God. The all-powerful God is stirred to action by our prayers. He knows all things but will withhold certain miracles and activities until we pray and seek Him. God told Moses that He had seen and heard and felt the affliction of the Hebrew slaves in Egypt but waited and waited until their cries burdened Him and He could not hold back (Judges 10:16). Intercession activates heaven. It is the on ramp for the heavenly super highway of miracles. Prayer releases power to the earth. What a mystery!

According to Genesis 2, God created man with a will, he ability to decide and determine his future. God has a will, and man has a will. Whenever man's will is not in agreement with God's will, God is limited. Man's will affects God's plan and purposes. The Church of Jesus Christ can extend God's kingdom or delay the coming of that kingdom.

When the Church places its will under God, He will move on earth the same way He will move in eternity. If we do not oppose God here, then heaven's will is done on earth. When the Church decides, God acts. The Lord wants a Bridal Partner, a help-mate that will work with Him as co-laborers with God (II Cor.6:1).

Sowing and Reaping in Prayer

The incredible principle of sowing and reaping applies to prayer in ways many do not comprehend. This is not only a principle for finances but it is also a foundational principle for the spirit energized life.

In Isaiah 61:11 God promises that righteousness and praise will spring forth from the earth in the sight of all the nations. This is a prophetic promise of the glorious church arising in holy partnership with her Bridegroom-King. This prophetic word must come to pass. God's purposes will surely blossom and come forth just as the spring brings new growth in the gardens of earth. BUT something has to be sown first; something must first be planted if it is to spring forth! Only what has been planted in the earth will bud to new life. There has to be a human partnership with God in planting seeds of righteousness and praise if they are to spring up and bring light to the nations. God needs His children to plant the right seeds so that the earth brings forth the right fruit. We have to sow righteousness and praise before the nations if we are to reap of the same kind.

Listen: The future state of a glorious church releasing light and power to the nations depends upon watchmen on earth who will never be silent and give God no rest until He makes His promise a living thing. This is ordained prayer. This is sowing prayer that will reap a harvest of righteousness. Where there is no one to partner with God in prayer, righteousness is not found, and the nations perish. There must be a high level of cooperation with the intent of God and the activity of the Church to accomplish the cosmic goals we seek. This exhilarating prayer will not grow silent until the light of glory shines upon us!

Becoming a prayer partner with Jesus Christ is the goal of intercession. We work together with God to determine the affairs of men – even future events. If we learn to pray with Jesus, breathing out His prayers on the earth, we can shape history. Think of Joshua commanding the sun to stand still. God needed his prayer to work that miracle.

In a way, everything God wants to do on earth He wants man to work with Him in bringing it to pass.

Father God is preparing a bridal partner for His Son who will reign together with Him. We become the voice of the Lord and the scepter of righteousness in His hand. The high priests of the Old Testament entered the Holy Place alone, but our Great High Priest begs us to come and be partners with Him in the Holy of Holies.

The Father has given His Son to be the Head over the Church. He is the Head; we are the Body (I Cor. 12:27). Yet, the Head cannot say to the rest of the body, "I don't need you" (I Cor. 12:21). Jesus needs His body to fulfill the plans of the Father. All of the destiny of the universe is waiting for the Head and the body to flow as one and fully express the nature of the Father... Then Jesus will have a place to "lay His head." See Luke 9:58.

Shapers of the Future

Prayer is the power that shapes the future, moving God to fulfill what is promised and stirring earth to respond to heaven. The future belongs to the intercessors. They are the ones who exercise spiritual defiance over what is seen and insist on a new inevitability in the affairs of earth. With the politics of hope, intercessors are filled with a vision of what *can be* if they pray.

The future belongs to whoever can envision it. A desirable possibility is held out for us in the gospel of Christ. God *will* intervene in all the affairs of earth, if intercessors will pray. A heavenly partnership is required, earth agreeing with heaven. This prayer of agreement releases the dreamed of future, helping to create the reality that is hoped for. Will you be a shaper of the future? Will you lock arms with Jesus and partner with Him?

God longs for an earth being to agree with Him. As we take our place on the sea of glass, as a human before

Deity's throne, the true purpose of creation falls into place. God has a representative and a partner on earth that will exercise dominion over what needs to be changed. It is our supreme task as intercessors to enter into this alliance with the throne room, calling out of the future the longed-for new present: "Thy kingdom come, thy will be done. On earth, like it is here on the sea of glass."

Prayer does more than meet the needs of men—it meets the needs of God. The Lord longs for a partner to join Him in prayer. By uniting our hearts in the prayer of agreement (earth + heaven), God's desired future is released from the throne. When God's Name is hallowed God's kingdom comes and His will is done. We hallow His name by agreeing with Him and worshipping the God who stoops to hear the prayers of His people.

Jesus came to do the will of the Father. Prayer is YOU doing the will of the Father. Jesus taught us that the priority of prayer is the will of God—the need of God to have one on earth agree with Him and implement His purposes. This is our destiny.

Intercession changes earth and releases the fulfillment of heaven's promises. Prayer will change us, but prayer must change the future, changing what is possible to what is real. Through prayer, God is permitted to act without violating human freedom. He has found a gateway to move through. Prayer is the way His will is escorted to the earth. This is why He implores us to ask, search, and knock. These imperative commands must be fulfilled if God is to fully implement divine strategies in a fallen world. We have been commanded to command.

We have been required to insist for intervention, asking for the sick, the poor, the lost, and the weak. Prayer is, in a sense, ordering God to bring His kingdom near. It is using authority to conform the present to the desirable future. Adoration will lead to intercession. Our worship will bring us to the place of knocking on closed doors until they fling open and kingdom power floods the earth.

Prayer rattles God's cage. It wakes Him up and stirs Him to action. It sets God free to act on our behalf. It is sending a letter to heaven's celestial capital where it is sorted, read, and responded to. Our words become powerful, like God's words when He created light from darkness. Our prayer words have power as a co-creator with God to shape the future together as prayer partners.

What if you were gripped with this reality? Would you want to pray more for His kingdom to come to the devastated places on earth? Far from being passive, prayer becomes a means of creating action where there is nothing but darkness. Our prayer voice becomes a trumpet that heralds what God is about to do. Perhaps *we* are those angels that hurl coals of fire from off the altar to the earth by means of fervent prayer (Rev. 9).

The God-Man Partnership

There is no clearer example of the divine partnership than the incarnation of the Christ. The eternal Son of God became a man—God with us (God partnering with humanity). At last, the Father has a Man that will partner with Him for the earth.

The plan of God has been from the beginning to mingle Himself with man and be one with Him forever. This forever partnership will be fulfilled, as we become His New Jerusalem Dwelling Place, His Bridal City. His Bride-to-be must learn on earth all she can about this divine partnership that is about to be unveiled.

The Son of God/Son of Man is heaven's prototype of a new species of new creation humanity, God and man partnering together to bring heaven to earth.

In heaven right now, the Man Christ Jesus is ever living to make intercession for us; that is, He is constantly—together with the Father—speaking over us the truth of who we are in Him. He has as His constant focus the declaration of agreement with the Father that we are His Bride, full and complete, the entire focus of His affections, and that in His sacrificial life, death, resurrection, and ascension He has poured out upon us all that we need for the divine nature to be completed in us, not only corporately, but individually as well.

Contemplative prayer is the consideration of *His* beauty that we might come to fully understand our own beauty and value to Him. And the wonder of it is that as we focus on Him, as we engage our voices and spirits to release the power of His Word interiorly, we become more enamored with His beauty and less concerned about ours, even as He makes us more beautiful in the process. This is the mutual admiration society of the heavenly marriage: Jesus selflessly ministers unto us in order to present us to Himself as His radiant Bride, "without spot or wrinkle."

The Branch of the Lord

It is almost inconceivable what the Lord has done for you. He has made it easy for you to pray. You come to pray before His throne, seated as His prince/princess—with privileges granted only to royalty. This truth was also revealed to Zechariah, the prophet: *"The word of the Lord came to me: 'Take silver and gold....and make a crown, and set it on the head of the high priest, JOSHUA'"* (Zech. 6:9-11).

Zechariah was instructed by God to crown a priest with a king's crown of gold and silver. And of all the names, the name of the high priest in that year was JOSHUA. Joshua is the Hebrew name for JESUS. There is a priest who is a king before God, JESUS.

The Body of Yeshua, Jesus, is His Church—you and I. Jesus has two bodies, one in heaven and one on earth. We are His corporate, many membered Body. We are a "Joshua company" of priests who are kings, kings who are priests.

> *Tell him [Joshua] this is what the LORD Almighty says: "Here is the man whose name is the Branch, and he [they] will branch out from His place [the Church, His dwelling place] and build the Temple of the Lord [the Church, His habitation - Eph. 2:22]. It is He who will build the Temple of the Lord, and He [they] will be clothed with majesty and will SIT [Eph. 2:6] and RULE on His throne. And He [they] will be a priest [a priest-hood] ON HIS THRONE."*
>
> Zechariah 6:12-13

There is a prophecy in the Old Testament book of Zechariah that tells us of a day when the **branch man** (Jesus the Vine *and* the Church, His branches) will spring forth in power and glory to build (become) the Temple of the Lord. We are His Temple, we are branches in His vine-life, we are priests who sit on a throne as the "Joshua company" of end time intercessors.

"The branch of the Lord" is understood by nearly every serious Bible student as a term for the Messiah, the Lord Jesus Christ. He is the Righteous Branch (Jer. 23:5-6) that springs forth with an ever-increasing life. This is **the Immanuel character** of Christ that increases and grows like a branch carrying His life of fruitfulness (Isa. 4:2, 9:6-7).

The yoke of Jesus (Matt. 11:28-30) is a yoke of *union*, not toilsome labor. It is the blending of the human and the divine. This is what took place in the manger. The God-Man was born as a prototype for a coming people. Our Lord Jesus took this yoke when He was born a man. Now, Jesus extends a yoke to His Church, a yoke of union with Him. It is a yoke of divine partnering in the affairs of heaven.

Earth is invited to rule with heaven, into a holy ONEness. This is where God wants us to go as we approach the wedding feast of the Lamb and His wife. It is a cooperative prayer initiative—you and God in a holy "co-op."

It is the purpose of God to make you into a "look-alike" of Jesus Christ. Reflecting His image, flowing in His power, praying His prayers.

The day will come when you will be able to say, like David said, **"I am a man of prayer"** (Psalm 109:4). The Hebrew text actually says, *"I am prayer!"* God will have a people who have *become* prayer. To hold Him as the Redeemer makes us the redeemed. You cannot separate the person from the prayer; they both are on fire. To pray as His partner will one day make you—**prayer!**

Who are these prayer partners with Jesus? They volunteer for everything and do it as for the Lord Himself. They study their Bibles and not tell everybody. They pray when no one is looking. They grin all the time even when people misunderstand. They can be faithful around difficult people, even submit to an imperfect leadership. They value the eternal over the temporary. They measure their days and take advantage of opportunities to live Christ day and night. They have nothing to gain, nothing to lose, nothing to prove, nothing to hide. They are becoming prayer partners with Jesus, being prepared for ruling with

Jesus for all eternity. Does that sound like something YOU would care to be involved with?

Beloved, It is time to become a prayer partner with Jesus!

---

[1] Ephesians 5:18 and Jude 20

Suggested Reading:

The Power of Prayer — E.M. Bounds

Developing Your Secret Closet of Prayer – Richard Burr

The Mighty Warrior — Elizabeth Alves

Surprised by the Voice of God — Jack Deere

The Power of Prayer and Fasting — Ronnie Floyd

The Lost Art of Intercession — Jim Goll

Rees Howells, Intercessor — Norman Grubb

Experiencing God Through Prayer — Jeanne Guyon

The Ministry of Intercession — Andrew Murray

Prayer: Asking & Receiving — John R. Rice

Hippo in the Garden — James Ryle

Praying with Power — C. Peter Wagner

Song of Songs — Brian Simmons

The Transforming Power of Prayer — James Houston

Intercessory Prayer — Dutch Sheets

The Fire of God — Michael Brown

Passion for Jesus — Mike Bickle

Beyond the Veil — Alice Smith

Cross-Pollination — Lila Terhune

Invading the Privacy of God — Cecil Murphey

Kneeling on the Promises – Jim Goll

Seasons of Intercession – Frank DaMazio

Needless Casualties of War – John Paul Jackson

Informed Intercession – George Otis Jr.

Winning the Prayer War – Kjell Sjoberg

Spiritual Warfare – Timothy Warner

The Fire of Delayed Answers – Bob Sorge

Praying Hyde – E.G. Carre

Time to Weep – Steve Hill

The Power of Brokenness – Don Nori

Listen, God Is Speaking to You – Quin Sherrer

Acts 29 Blueprint for the House of Prayer – Terry Teykl

Three Battlegrounds – Francis Frangipane

The Hour That Changes the World – Dick Eastman

Father, Forgive Us – Jim Goll

Your Kingdom Come – Michael Sullivant

Hearing God – Dallas Willard

The Watchman – Tom Hess

Wasted on Jesus — Jim Goll

God.com – James Alexander Langteaux

Destined for the Throne – Paul Billheimer

The Soul's Sincere Desire – Glen Clark

Moving God through Prayer – Zacharias Tanee Fomom

Lessons on Prayer – Witness Lee

The Breaker Anointing — Barbara Yoder

The Powers That Be – Walter Wink

Governmental Prayer – Noel Woodroffe

Incense and Thunder – Dudley Hall

Author Information

Brian & Candy Simmons have been in active ministry for over twenty-five years. They have served as tribal missionaries planting churches among the Kuna people of Panama, where they assisted in the translation of the New Testament into the native language. While in the jungle, they were visited by the Holy Spirit in a revival that brought many native people to salvation in Jesus Christ. Brian has authored a number of books that focus on the prophetic purposes of God for this emerging generation. They are convinced that God's Spirit will be poured out in revival power upon the nations of the earth, including the United States and New England, before the return of our Lord Jesus.

The passion of their ministry has been to equip this generation to become radical lovers of Jesus Christ and to make Him famous in the nations of the earth. They oversee a growing family of churches in New England, helping others to find their place of ministry in the Body of Christ. Brian is also the Sr. Pastor of Gateway Christian Fellowship in West Haven, Connecticut where they make their home. They are blessed with three children and three grandchildren.

Other Books by Brian Simmons:

GENESIS: *The Spiritual Seed & the Ways of God*

PRAYER PARTNER WITH JESUS: *Secrets of Intercession*

DAVIDIC WORSHIP: *David, His Tabernacle & His Psalms*

SONGS OF SONGS — THE JOURNEY OF THE BRIDE:
*The inspired allegory of Divine romance between Christ and
His Bride, the Church*

For more information on Stairway Ministries and a complete listing of their teaching materials, contact:

Stairway Ministries
P.O.Box 26512
West Haven, CT. 06516
U.S.A.
www.stairwayministries.org